RUSSIAN DECLENSION AND CONJUGATION:

1.95

D1113232

5/232

Have to know lists of
exceptions?
short form adj;
abnormal stress shifts

RUSSIAN DECLENSION AND CONJUGATION:

A STRUCTURAL DESCRIPTION WITH EXERCISES

Maurice I. Levin

1978

Slavica Publishers, Inc.

Columbus, Ohio

For a complete catalog of Slavica books, with prices and ordering information, write to:

Slavica Publishers, Inc.
P.O. Box 14388
Columbus, Ohio 43214

ISBN: 0-89357-048-6

Copyright © 1978 by Maurice I. Levin. All rights reserved.

Editor of Slavica Publishers, Inc.: Charles E. Gribble, The Ohio State University, Columbus.

Printed in the United States of America by Thomson-Shore, Inc., Dexter, Michigan 48130.

To my family

PREFACE

The aim of this book is to present the essentials
of Russian declension and conjugation as succinctly, yet
as completely, as possible in the hope of demonstrating
the fundamental simplicity and order to be found in Russian grammar. The material presented in this book was
originally used in a course on the structure of Russian
for teachers and beginning graduate students at Indiana
University in 1965, and it has been undergoing continu-
al expansion and revision since that time. While the
book may best be utilized at that level, it has also
been used at several universities in courses of advanced
language study and has been found to be an effective
tool for reviewing and solidifying a student's understanding of declension and conjugation.

Since this book is designed for use at various
levels, there may be times when the exercises are too
simple for one level or too difficult for another. For
this reason, the instructor will have to be ready to
make adjustments in either direction by explaining those
exercises that create difficulties and by eliminating or
expanding those that are not sufficiently challenging.

The book is divided into two major parts: declension (Chapters 2-5) and conjugation (Chapters 6-8).
Chapter 1 presents an introduction to structural (i.e.,
simplified morphophonemic) transcription that is crucial
to an understanding of the presentation of declension
and conjugation. (Therefore, until the material of that
chapter is clear, no attempt should be made to proceed
beyond it.) In presenting declension and conjugation,
the major attempt has been to demonstrate the order and
regularity in Russian grammar, in the hope that once it
is clear what is *regular*, the student will no longer
need to be told what is *irregular*. (Chapter 9 does contain a catalogue of the major irregularities in both the
noun and the verb, but in a sense the student ought to
be able to do that on his/her own.) A second, more important, goal is to show that a great deal of what is
often considered irregular in Russian grammar is not irregular at all, but only badly presented.

Much of the material in this book can be found in other sources (see acknowledgments below). There are, however, two major contributions which the book offers: (1) this material is brought together in a single volume; and (2) the treatment of noun and adjective stress patterns represents a new synthesis based on previously unobserved relationships. There is also a fuller listing of irregularities in imperfective derivation than has been available up to now, and the analysis of the fill vowel in declension is both simple and complete, yet reasonably free of exceptions.

ACKNOWLEDGMENTS

The presentation of structural transcription in Chapter 1, as well as the basic notion of a single set of declensional endings, owes a great deal to Morris Halle's "Essay on the Relationship between Russian Sounds and Letters," in B. A. Lapidus and S. V. Shevtsova, *The Learner's Russian-English Dictionary* (Cambridge, Mass.: The M.I.T. Press [c. 1963]), 681-88. The treatment of conjugation and of imperfective derivation is based largely on the work of Alexander Lipson as it appears in his textbook, *A Russian Course*, 2nd prelim. ed., (Cambridge, Mass.: Slavica, 1974). I have also made use of certain concepts outlined by Charles Townsend in his treatment of the verb in *Russian Word-Formation* (New York: McGraw-Hill, 1970). To both Lipson and Townsend I am indebted not only for ideas borrowed from their works, but also for a great deal of stimulating discussion on the presentation and analysis of Russian grammar.

I would also like to express considerable gratitude to Charles Gribble for his advice and encouragement. I am also grateful to Frank Ingram, Michael Launer, Anny Newman, Lawrence Newman, and Rodney Sangster for using these materials in various stages of completeness and for their many useful comments about them. Other valuable suggestions have come from Robert Beard, Richard Brecht, Catherine Chvany, Dan Davidson, Joseph Lake, Michael Rosenbush, and Robert Rothstein, and to all of them I express sincere gratitude. A special note of thanks is also offered to Dean Jeremiah Allen of the University of Massachusetts for his assistance.

Most of all I would like to thank all of my students for the many valuable suggestions, corrections,

and opinions which they have offered over the past doz-
en years that these materials have been used in the
classroom. To all of them I express my warmest appreci-
tion.

This work was funded in part by a grant from the
Research Council of the University of Massachusetts.

                          Maurice I. Levin
January 1978

CONTENTS

CHAPTER ONE

STRUCTURAL TRANSCRIPTION

The declension of Russian substantives (nouns, adjectives, and pronominal adjectives) can be shown to be a simple phenomenon when viewed not in terms of the Russian orthography (spelling system), but in the light of a system of transcription which will be called *structural transcription*, or ST. There are certain features, hidden or distorted by the orthography, which are much more easily explained and understood when treated in the framework of the ST.

There are in Russian certain basic vowel and consonant sounds which are rendered, as in many languages, by the spelling system. However, like any spelling system, the Russian system for indicating these basic units is not perfect. In the discussion that follows we will compare the basic units (indicated in the ST by Latin letters) with the units of the spelling system (indicated by Cyrillic letters) in order to point out where the spelling system causes confusion. It will be important to distinguish at all times the basic units (consonant and vowel *sounds*) from the units of the spelling system (consonant and vowel *letters*).

It should also be noted at this time that the ST is not a phonetic transcription. A phonetic transcription is one which attempts to reduce to written form *all* of the elements in the sound system of the language, to approximate through written symbols exactly what is heard when a Russian utterance is produced. The ST, on the other hand, records the *basic* sound units, and the key word here is "basic."

A basic unit is a kind of abstract structural element, and every language is made up of a limited number of these elements. As stated above, the spelling system is the traditional method of recording these elements, but it is seldom a very efficient vehicle. In the case of Russian, the spelling system is more efficient than that of many other languages, and for this reason there will be many instances when it seems that the ST is not unlike a system of transliteration. (Transliteration is a means of representing elements of one writing system by using those of another, for example, using Latin letters to render words or names that are normally written in a non-Latin system such as Cyrillic, Arabic, Hebrew, etc.) But since the spelling system does contain certain inadequacies and distortions, we will attempt to look beyond it at the structural elements, and the ST will provide us with the tool to accomplish this.

The Russian alphabet contains 33 letters: 10 vowel letters, 21 consonant letters, and 2 signs of separation. The inventory of basic sound units, however, totals 38 items: 5 vowel units and 33 consonant units. The consonants may be either hard or soft, and this distinction is crucial for an understanding of the relationship between the basic sound units and the letters that represent them.

The five basic vowel units and the ten vowel letters used to represent them are as follows:

Basic vowel units	Vowel letters Group I	Vowel letters Group II
a	а	я
e	э	е
i	ы	и
o	о	ё
u	у	ю

The thirty-three basic consonant units may be divided into two types, paired and unpaired. The paired consonants are those whose hardness or softness is independent of the environment; the unpaired consonants are those whose hardness or softness is predetermined either by the environment or by the nature of the consonant itself. It can be seen in the chart on the following page that in the case of the paired consonants a single consonant letter is used to represent either of two basic consonant sounds, since each related hard and soft pair is written with the same consonant letter. In the ST the softness of the paired consonants will be indicated by a hook ( ) under the letter.

Basic consonant units   Consonant letters

(Paired)

d	d̨	t	t̨	Д		Т
b	b̨	p	p̨	б		П
z	z̨	s	s̨	з		с
v	v̨	f	f̨	в		ф
m	m̨	n	n̨	М		Н
r	r̨	l	l̨	р		Л

(Unpaired)

k	g	x	К	Г	Х
š	ž	c	Ш	Ж	Ц
č	šč	j	Ч	Щ	Й

The discussion of what happens when we combine basic units will be divided into two main parts: (1) consonant plus vowel; (2) consonant not followed by a vowel.

A. CONSONANT PLUS VOWEL

1. PAIRED CONSONANT PLUS VOWEL. The combination of a paired consonant plus vowel is rendered in Russian spelling in the following ways:

a. HARD PAIRED CONSONANT PLUS VOWEL. This combination is always written with the appropriate consonant letter plus a vowel letter from Group I.

zavódu   завóду

voróta   ворóта

borodá   бородá

   b. SOFT PAIRED CONSONANT PLUS VOWEL. This
combination is always written with the appropriate consonant letter plus a vowel letter from Group II.

   ņeďéļu   неде́лю

   ťóťa   тётя

   ļiśé   лисе́

EXERCISES

Combining paired consonants and vowels.

1. Rewrite the following forms in Cyrillic:

   a. ďéťi   f. poródi

   b. músora   g. podúmaļi

   c. záņati   h. ņeņála

   d. napisáļi   i. pólosi

   e. ļúḥiťe   j. upaďóťe

2. Rewrite the following forms in ST:

   a. вари́ли   f. литерату́ра

   b. зовёте   g. ребя́та

   c. сéмя   h. молоды́ми

   d. дя́ди   i. лю́ди

   e. заво́ды   j. полёты

   2. UNPAIRED CONSONANT PLUS VOWEL. The combination of an unpaired consonant plus vowel follows a somewhat different pattern and may be summarized as follows:

a. VELAR PLUS VOWEL. Even though the velars (k, g, x) may be either hard or soft, they are classed as unpaired consonants because the hardness or softness is dependent upon the following vowel. That is, unlike the truly paired consonants which may be either hard or soft before any of the five basic vowel units,[1] the velars are always hard before a, o, or u and always soft before e or i. The only exceptions to this occur in a few marginal verb forms and will not materially affect the relevance of this statement for declension. Thus the combination of a velar with a, o, or u is always written with the appropriate consonant letter plus a vowel letter from Group I, while the combination of a velar with e or i is written with a consonant letter plus a vowel letter from Group II.

nogá	НОГá	nógi	НóГИ
rúku	рýКУ	ruké	рУКé
múxoj	МýХОЙ	múxi	МýХИ

Note that no hook appears under the velar consonant before e or i, since the softness here is automatic.

EXERCISES

Combining velar consonants and vowels.

1. Rewrite the following forms in Cyrillic:

a. goloví *головы*   f. nógu *ногу*

b. bloxé *блохе*   g. suxími *сухими*

c. púxa *пуха*   h. visokó *высоко́*

d. şekí *секи*   i. kínuļi *кинули*

e. ŗokíţe *покити*   j. dorógi *дороги*

---

[1]Except that no hard paired consonant ever appears before the basic vowel e in words of native Russian origin.

2. Rewrite the following forms in ST:

a. ре́ки *réki*   f. доро́ге *doroge*

b. города́ *goroda*   g. высока́ *visoká*

c. му́хе *muxe*   h. за́сухи *zasuxi*

d. купи́те *kupíte*   i. пироги́ *pirogí*

e. нога́ми *nogami*   j. гуля́ка *gulaka*

     b. HUSHER PLUS VOWEL. The hushing conso-
nants, or hushers (š, ž, č, šč), unlike the velars,
are completely unaffected by the vowel that follows
them, since they can only be hard (š, ž) or soft (č,
šč). Like the velars, however, the combination of consonant plus the vowel a or u is written with the appropriate consonant letter plus a vowel letter from
Group I, and the combination of consonant plus the vowel e or i is written with a consonant letter plus a
vowel letter from Group II. The combination of husher
plus the vowel o merits special attention.

     In a root the combination of husher plus o is
spelled with a vowel letter from either Group I or Group
II. [1] In a declensional ending, however, the choice of
vowel letter is dependent upon the place of stress.
That is, if the o is stressed it is spelled with a vowel
letter from Group I (O); if unstressed it is spelled
with the corresponding vowel letter from Group II (ë).
Note, however, that since in the latter instance we are
dealing with unstressed position, the letter ë is replaced by the letter e.

_____

[1] A Group I vowel letter will be used in those
instances when stress remains on that syllable in all
forms of the paradigm or in all related words (i.e.,
words with the same root), e.g., шо́рох, чо́порный,
шо́ры, etc. However, when stress moves to another syllable, either within the paradigm or in related words,
then a vowel letter from Group II is used, e.g., шёпот
(because of шепта́ть), щёлок (because of щелочно́й),
жёлоб (because of the plural желоба́), etc.

For example:

čáša	ча́ша	čáši	ча́ши
dušá	душа́	duší	души́
čášu	ча́шу	čáše	ча́ше
dúšu	ду́шу	dušé	душе́

but

čášoj	ча́шей	dušój	душо́й

EXERCISES

Combining hushers and vowels.

1. Rewrite the following forms in Cyrillic:

   a. káša   *кawa* *KAŠa*   f. vášu   *ва́шу* *VÁŠu*

   b. xorošó   *хорошо́* *xorošóg.*   g. ščúki   *щу́ки* *ščúki*

   c. noží   *ножи* *noží*   h. žíteli   (*жители*) *ziťeli*

   d. tóščomu   *то́щему* *tóščomu i.*   i. xoróšogo   *хоро́шего* *xoróšogo*

   e. lúže   *луже* *lúže*   j. čužómu   *чужо́му* *čužómu*

2. Rewrite the following forms in ST:

   a. на́ши   *náši*   f. ножа́   *nožá*

   b. часа́ми   *časámi*   g. чита́ли   *čitáli*

   c. ро́жу   *róžu*   h. ве́щи   *véšči*

   d. чужо́го   *čužógo*   i. ка́шу   *kášu*

   e. меже́   *mežé*   j. хоро́шему *xoróšomu*

c. THE CONSONANT *c* PLUS VOWEL. The spelling of the combination of the consonant *c* with the vowels *a*, *u*, and *e* follows the same rules as for the combination of hushers with these vowels. The same is true of the combination of *c* plus *o* in a declensional ending. The combination of *c* with the vowel *i* in a declensional ending, however, is written with the consonant letter plus a vowel letter from Group I (Ы), while in a root, vowel letters from both groups are found. (The Group I vowel letter is found in native Russian words, while a Group II letter appears in words of foreign origin, e.g., цыплёнок, but цифра.)

ņémca	НЕ́МЦА	*ņémca*	otcá	ОТЦА́	*otcá*
ņémcu	НЕ́МЦУ	*ņémcu*	otcú	ОТЦУ́	*otcú*
ņémce	НЕ́МЦЕ	*ņémce*	otcé	ОТЦЕ́	*otce*
ņémci	НЕ́МЦЫ	*ņémci*	otcí	ОТЦЫ́	*otcí*

but

ņémcom	НЕ́МЦЕМ	*ņémcom*	otcóm	ОТЦО́М	*otcóm*
ņémcov	НЕ́МЦЕВ	*ņémcov*	otcóv	ОТЦО́В	*otcóv*

EXERCISES

The combination of *c* with vowels.

1. Rewrite the following forms in Cyrillic:

a. ļicó   лицо́ *ļicó*   d. şérdca   сердца *sérdca*

b. tánci   танцы *tánci*   e. ļicé   лице *ļicé*

c. vincú   винцы *vincú*   f. şérdcom   сердцем *s'érgcom*

2. Rewrite the following forms in ST:

a. ВИНЦО́М *vincóm*   c. ТА́НЦЕВ *táncov*

b. УЧЕНИ́ЦЫ *učeņíci*   d. ЛИЦУ́ *ļicu*

učeņíti

d. THE CONSONANT *j* PLUS VOWEL. In Sections A,1,b and A,2 it was pointed out that a Group II vowel letter preceded directly by a consonant letter indicates that the preceding consonant, if paired, is soft, and if unpaired, that the choice of vowel letter is an orthographical convention. When a Group II vowel letter appears in a position *not* directly preceded by a consonant letter (i.e., in initial position, or following a vowel or one of the signs of separation), it indicates the combination of *j* plus vowel.

jáma	яма	dajót	даёт	*dajot*
jéļi	ели	čitájut	читáют	*čitajut*
jólka	ёлка	stojít	стойт	*stojıt*
júbka	юбка	stoját	стоят	*stojat*
jéxal	ехал	saráje	сарáе	*saráje*

A major exception to the rule stated above concerns the letter и at the beginning of a word. In that position the letter и does not signal the presence of the consonant *j*. For example, игрá and идéя are to be rendered in ST as *igrá* and *iḍéja*.

EXERCISES

The combination of *j* with vowels.

1. Rewrite the following forms in Cyrillic:

    a. pojóțe поёте *nojome*   d. kajúta каюта *kajuta*

    b. mojími мошми *mojımi*   e. mojá моя *mojá*

    c. jéxaļi ехали *jexaļi*   f. géņijov ченнев *géņijov*

2. Rewrite the following forms in ST:

    a. пойте *nojițe*   c. языки *jazıkí*

    b. надоели *nadojeļi*   d. якорю *jakoŗu*

B.   CONSONANT NOT FOLLOWED BY VOWEL

1.   PAIRED CONSONANTS

a.   HARD PAIRED CONSONANTS. Hard paired consonants not followed by a vowel are written with the appropriate consonant letter only, nothing more.

zavód	завóд	kómnata	кóмната
slón	слóн	vóln	вóлн

b.   SOFT PAIRED CONSONANTS. Soft paired consonants not followed by a vowel are written with the appropriate consonant letter followed by the soft sign.

tól̦ko	тóлько	króv̦	крóвь
n̦ed̦él̦	недéль	pról̦ba	прóсьба

2.   UNPAIRED CONSONANTS

Unpaired consonants not followed by a vowel
are generally written with just the appropriate consonant
letter and nothing more. This is true for the velars, *c*,
and *j*, and no special problems arise.

kn̦íg	кни́г	mój	мóй
blóx	блóх	str̦ígla	стри́гла
vólk	вóлк	bácnuț	бáцнуть
oțéc	отéц	čájka	чáйка

The above statement also applies to the hush-
ing consonants, except that in certain instances a soft
sign must be written following a husher. These instances
are:

a.   the second person singular, nonpast tense,
of all Russian verbs;

кладёшь   говори́шь

   b. the imperative;

   ре́жь, ре́жьте   плачь, пла́чьте

   c. the nominative and accusative singular of
feminine nouns ending in -∅;

   но́чь   ро́жь

   ве́щь   мы́шь

   d. the infinitive;

   мо́чь   пе́чь

   e. certain adverbs.

   про́чь   сплóшь

   на́стежь   то́чь-в-то́чь

   In all of the above instances we are dealing
with an orthographical convention, a spelling rule, and
nothing more.

EXERCISES

Consonants not followed by a vowel.

1. Rewrite the following forms in Cyrillic:

   a. boļnój больно́й   f. jéšţe (*imperative*) е́шьте

   b. jájca яйца   g. končáţ конча́ть

   c. ţuŗmí тюрьмы   h. áxnuţ а́хнуть

   d. továŗišč това́рищ   i. kúxoŋ ку́хонь

   e. ukraḑóš (*2nd sg,*   j. stŗíč (*infinitive*)
         nonpast)   стричь
       украдёшь

2. Rewrite the following forms in ST:

a. ОТЕ́Ц   *oțéc*   ~~otéc~~   f. ГОЛО́В *golóv*   *golóv*

b. ЗОВЁШЬ *zov̦óš* ~~zovóš~~   g. ВЕ́ЩЬ *v̦ešč*   *v̦ešč*

c. БОЛЬШО́Й *bol̦šoj* ~~bol̦šoj~~   h. МА́ЖЬТЕ *mažțe*   *mažțe*

d. СУДЬБА́ *sud̦bá* ~~sud̦bá~~   i. ИГРА́ТЬ *igráț'*   *igráț'*

e. ЗА́ЙЦЫ *zájci* ~~zájci~~   j. ЗДА́НИЙ *zdánij*   *zdánij*

C. THE SIGNS OF SEPARATION

1. HARD SIGN. The hard sign has a single function in Russian, to separate a prefix ending in a consonant from a root which begins with *j*. For example:

prefix *ot* + *jéxaț* = *otjéxaț* (ОТЪѢ́ХАТЬ)

prefix *s*   + *jésț* = *sjésț* (СЪѢ́СТЬ)

prefix *ob* + *javíț* = *objavíț* (ОБЪЯВИ́ТЬ)

2. SOFT SIGN. Aside from its use in indicating
the softness of a paired consonant not followed by a
vowel (B,1,b) or after a husher in certain forms (B,2),
the soft sign is used to separate a consonant from a
following *j* everywhere except at the boundary between
prefix and root, where the hard sign is used.

p̦jót	ПЬЁТ	b̦jú	БЬЮ
șemjá	СЕМЬЯ́	sud̦jé	СУДЬЕ́
tṛéțji	ТРЕ́ТЬИ	staț jój	СТАТЬЕ́Й
šjóm	ШЬЁМ	ružjó	РУЖЬЁ́
čjú	ЧЬЮ	čjéj	ЧЬЕ́Й
p̦ján	ПЬЯ́Н	šjút	ШЬЮ́Т
čjó	ЧЬЁ	v̦éščju	ВЕ́ЩЬЮ

EXERCISES

The signs of separation.

1. Rewrite the following forms in Cyrillic:

   a. objéxaţ _объѣхать_   f. báhji _бабьи_

   b. sobáčja _собачья_   g. sjézdiţ _съѣздить_

   c. uhjót _убьём_   h. tŗéţjogo _третьего_

   d. solovjí _соловьи_   i. sudjú _судью_

   e. ručjú _ручью_   j. skaŋjá _скамья_

2. Rewrite the following forms in ST:

   a. льёт _l'jut_   f. чьих _čjix_

   b. объём _objom_   g. дверью _dver'ju_

   c. семьé _sem'é_   h. лисья _lišja_

   d. трéтьими _trétjimi_   i. допьёте _dopjoťe_

   e. подъезжáют _podezzajut_   j. соловья _solovjá_

QUESTIONS FOR THOUGHT AND DISCUSSION

1. How does the Russian alphabet distort the actual situation regarding the basic consonant units?

2. Many grammar textbooks refer to hard and soft vowels, rather than consonants. Can you explain the popularity of this idea?

3. How many ways are there to write the basic consonant $\check{j}$ in Cyrillic? What are they?

4. How many ways are there to write the other basic consonant units?

5. Why is it not necessary to indicate the softness of the velars? Of the hushers *č* and *šč*? Of *j*?

6. Why is the letter э so seldom used?

7. Why is the letter е somewhat ambiguous with regard to the basic vowel units it may represent?

8. In what way does the letter и deviate from the pattern observed in the other vowel letters of Group II?

9. The hard and soft signs are often referred to as "signs of separation." Is this term accurate? What are the functions of the hard and soft signs?

D. CONCLUSION

We have seen that paired consonants are revealed to be either hard or soft in dependence upon the nature of the vowel letter that follows, and when not followed by a vowel letter, upon the presence or absence of the soft sign. For unpaired consonants the vowel letter provides no such information, since the choice of letter here is purely arbitrary. Two major areas of diversion from these basic rules are found in the spelling of the consonant *j* and of the vowel *o*.

When *j* is followed by a vowel it is written solely by means of a vowel letter from Group II, and when it is not followed by a vowel, by means of the appropriate consonant letter (й). When *j* is preceded by a consonant it is separated from that consonant by one of the signs of separation: by a hard sign at the boundary between prefix and root and by a soft sign anywhere else. Note that a paired consonant before *j* at the prefix-root boundary generally remains hard, while in any other position a paired consonant before *j* is always soft.

In spelling the vowel *o* in a declensional ending following a husher or *c*, the choice of vowel letter always depends upon the place of stress: о if stressed, е if unstressed. Since *j* plus unstressed *o* will also be spelled with the letter е, there are several instances when the letter е may be ambiguous with regard to whether it represents a basic *o* or *e*.

CHAPTER TWO

NOUN STRESS

A. INTRODUCTION

Before examining the problem of noun declension
it will be necessary to make some basic statements
about stress in nouns and about the system to be used
in designating the various patterns of noun stress.

Stress in Russian nouns may be either fixed on
the same syllable throughout the paradigm, or it may
be movable (i.e., it may shift to some other syllable
in certain declensional forms). With very few exceptions, if a shift occurs it will be from a syllable of
the stem to the ending or vice versa, and not from one
syllable of the stem to another.

B. THE THREE BASIC PATTERNS OF NOUN STRESS

There are three patterns of noun stress in
Russian: fixed, shifting, and anomalous. The first
type is by far the most numerous, but the other two
types occur in a large number of very common nouns.

1. FIXED STRESS

Nouns with fixed stress are those that have
stress on the same syllable in all forms of the singular and plural. Stress may fall either on a syllable
of the stem or on the endings, but in either case we
are dealing with two variants of the same pattern. The
symbol (') will be used to indicate the fixed stress
pattern and will be placed over that syllable of the
base form on which the stress falls. (Detailed information about the base form will be found in Section C
of Chapter 3. For now it will be sufficient to point
out that the base form very closely resembles the
nominative singular form of the noun written in ST
with other information added to enable the student to
generate all the forms of that noun.)

The following are some common nouns with fixed stress:

Stem stress	End stress
автобус	отец
книга	госпожа
чувство	этаж
товарищ	статья
неделя	

The following schemes give a more graphic representation of the two variants of this pattern. The symbol —— + — is used to indicate *stem plus ending*, i.e., the division of the word that is most relevant for an analysis of declension.

Fixed stem stress (——´— + —)

	Singular	Plural
N	—´— + —	—´— + —
A	—´— + —	—´— + —
G	—´— + —	—´— + —
P	—´— + —	—´— + —
D	—´— + —	—´— + —
I	—´— + —	—´— + —

Fixed end stress (—— + —´)

	Singular	Plural
N	—— + —´	—— + —´
A	—— + —´	—— + —´
G	—— + —´	—— + —´
P	—— + —´	—— + —´
D	—— + —´	—— + —´
I	—— + —´	—— + —´

2. SHIFTING STRESS

The second pattern of noun stress, the shifting pattern, involves an opposition between singular and

plural, whereby the stress is seen to shift either from
a syllable of the stem in all forms of the singular to
the ending in all forms of the plural, or to move back
one syllable from the ending in the singular to the
stem in the plural. Here, too, we are dealing with two
variants of the same pattern, and a single symbol ($^\times$)
may be used to indicate the appropriate variant, if we
place that symbol either over a syllable of the stem in
the base form or over the ending. That is, placing
this symbol over the stem in the base form indicates
that the singular forms of that noun will have stem
stress and that the plural forms will have end stress.
Placing the symbol over the ending in the base form
indicates the opposite, i.e., end stress in the singular
and stem stress in the plural.

Some common nouns with shifting stress are:

Stem to ending	Ending to stem
долг	число
город	вино
дело	жена
место	звезда

Stem to ending ($\underset{\times}{\rule{1cm}{0.4pt}} + -$)

	Singular	Plural
N	´— + —	—— + ´
A	´— + —	—— + ´
G	´— + —	—— + ´
P	´— + —	—— + ´
D	´— + —	—— + ´
I	´— + —	—— + ´

Ending to stem ($\rule{1cm}{0.4pt} + \underset{\times}{\rule{0.5cm}{0.4pt}}$)

	Singular	Plural
N	—— + ´	´— + —
A	—— + ´	´— + —
G	—— + ´	´— + —
P	—— + ´	´— + —
D	—— + ´	´— + —
I	—— + ´	´— + —

3. ANOMALOUS STRESS

The third pattern of stress involves an opposition within the plural, whereby the direct cases of the plural (i.e., nominative and inanimate accusative) are opposed to the oblique cases (genitive, prepositional, dative, instrumental). In the anomalous pattern the stress is always on the endings in the oblique cases of the plural and on the *first* syllable of the stem in the direct cases. Stress in the singular of these nouns may fall either on the first syllable of the stem or on the endings.

As in both the fixed and shifting patterns, the fact that we are dealing with two variants of the same pattern allows us to use a single symbol (`) for both variants, placing it either over the stem or the ending in the base form. Placing it over the stem indicates stem stress in the singular forms, while placing it over the ending signifies end stress. The plural of either variant, as noted above, has stress on the first syllable of the stem in the direct cases and on the endings in the oblique case forms.

Some common nouns with the anomalous stress pattern are:

Stem stress in sg.	End stress in sg.
бóг	кóнь
вóлк	губá
вéщь	слезá
двéрь	блохá

Stem stress in sg. (—́— + —)

	Singular	Plural
N	—́— + —	—́— + —
A	—́— + —	—́— + —
G	—́— + —	—— + —́
P	—́— + —	—— + —́
D	—́— + —	—— + —́
I	—́— + —	—— + —́

End stress in sg. (——— + ´)

	Singular	Plural
N	——— + ´	´——— + —
A	——— + ´	´——— + —
G	——— + ´	——— + ´
P	——— + ´	——— + ´
D	——— + ´	——— + ´
I	——— + ´	——— + ´

4.   THE *u*-RETRACTION

There is an additional subtype affecting only a small number of feminine nouns ending in -*á* that belong to either the shifting or anomalous pattern. This subtype exhibits a shift of stress to the stem in the accusative singular. (NB: For nouns of the anomalous pattern this means a shift to the *first* syllable of the stem, a fact which has significance, of course, only for nouns of more than two syllables.)

Since the ending -*u* is always involved in this shift, it will be referred to as the "*u*-retraction" and will be designated by [←] after the base form (e.g., *vod+á* [←] or *golov+á* [←]). There are only about thirteen nouns of the shifting pattern that have this retraction and about eighteen of the anomalous pattern. There is, however, some variation and wavering in certain of these nouns, with the result that sometimes two, three, or even four patterns of stress receive sanction in the reference books. For example, the preferred pattern for the noun река́ is *ṛek+á* [←], but there are three other permissible variants: *ṛek+á* [←], *ṛek+á*, *ṛek+á*.

Some common nouns with the *u*-retraction are:

Shifting	Anomalous	
вода́	борода́	среда́
душа́	голова́	стена́
земля́	гора́	сторона́
зима́	доска́	строка́
коса́	нога́	щека́
спина́	река́	
цена́	рука́	

Schematic representation of the *u*-retraction:

Shifting (——— + $\overset{\times}{\_}$ [←])

	Singular	Plural
N	——— + $\overset{\prime}{\_}$	$\overset{\prime}{\_\_}$ + —
A	$\overset{\prime}{\_\_}$ + —	$\overset{\prime}{\_\_}$ + —
G	——— + $\overset{\prime}{\_}$	$\overset{\prime}{\_\_}$ + —
P	——— + $\overset{\prime}{\_}$	$\overset{\prime}{\_\_}$ + —
D	——— + $\overset{\prime}{\_}$	$\overset{\prime}{\_\_}$ + —
I	——— + $\overset{\prime}{\_}$	$\overset{\prime}{\_\_}$ + —

Anomalous (——— + $\overset{\backsim}{\_}$ [←])

	Singular	Plural
N	——— + $\overset{\prime}{\_}$	$\overset{\prime}{\_\_}$ + —
A	$\overset{\prime}{\_\_}$ + —	$\overset{\prime}{\_\_}$ + —
G	——— + $\overset{\prime}{\_}$	——— + $\overset{\prime}{\_}$
P	——— + $\overset{\prime}{\_}$	——— + $\overset{\prime}{\_}$
D	——— + $\overset{\prime}{\_}$	——— + $\overset{\prime}{\_}$
I	——— + $\overset{\prime}{\_}$	——— + $\overset{\prime}{\_}$

EXERCISES

1. Divide the nouns listed on the following page into three groups depending upon whether they have fixed, shifting, or anomalous stress.

2. For the nouns of each basic pattern decide whether the symbol representing that pattern would be placed over the stem or the ending in the base form. Upon what will your decision be based?

3. Which of the nouns have the *u*-retraction?

	N sg	A sg	G sg	N pl	G pl	D pl
1.	зе́ркало	зе́ркало	зе́ркала	зеркала́	зерка́л	зеркала́м
2.	враг	врага́	врага́	враги́	враго́в	врага́м
3.	труба́	трубу́	трубы́	тру́бы	труб	тру́бам
4.	бровь	бровь	брови	брови	бровей	бровям
5.	гора́	го́ру	горы́	го́ры	гор	гора́м
6.	колесо́	колесо́	колеса́	колёса	колёс	колёсам
7.	зверь	зве́ря	зве́ря	зве́ри	звере́й	зверя́м
8.	вдова́	вдову́	вдовы́	вдо́вы	вдов	вдо́вам
9.	черта́	черту́	черты́	черты́	черт	черта́м
10.	душа́	ду́шу	души́	ду́ши	душ	ду́шам
11.	чай	чай	чая	чаи	чаёв	чаям
12.	строка́	строку́	строки́	стро́ки	строк	строка́м
13.	мост	мост	моста́	мосты́	мосто́в	моста́м
14.	гусь	гуся	гуся	гуси	гусей	гусям
15.	пляж	пляж	пляжа	пляжи	пляжей	пляжам
16.	сторона́	сто́рону	стороны́	сто́роны	сторо́н	сторона́м
17.	шкаф	шкаф	шкафа	шкафы	шкафов	шкафа́м
18.	степь	степь	степи	степи	степей	степям
19.	цена́	це́ну	цены́	це́ны	цен	це́нам
20.	сарай	сарай	сарая	сараи	сараев	сараям

C. ADDITIONAL COMMENTS

There are some additional comments that need to be included for the sake of completeness and clarity.

1. END STRESS

When it is stated that stress falls on an ending or shifts to an ending, there is no real ambiguity as to which syllable bears the stress, since almost all noun endings are monosyllabic. If it is understood as well that stress on an ending always implies stress on the *first* syllable of the ending, then there can be no possibility of ambiguity in the two disyllabic endings (the *I pl* ending *-aṃi* and the variant *I sg* ending *-oju*).

2. ZERO ENDING

Another general statement that may serve to eliminate confusion concerns the place of stress in a form with a zero ending. Since stress can actually fall on an ending only when that ending begins with a vowel, the true position of the stress in any form in which the ending does not begin with a vowel can be determined only in relation to the position of the stress in the other forms of the paradigm.

We can take as examples certain of the nouns in the exercise on the preceding page. The syllable which bears the stress in the *N sg* of Nos. 2 and 15 appears to be the same in each one, the vowel of the stem. Yet when we compare the other forms of each noun, it becomes apparent that only пляж is truly stem-stressed; враг is actually end-stressed, since all other forms of this noun have stress on the endings. A representation of the *N sg* of each noun in ST would indicate the difference between them (*pl̨áž+∅, vrag+∅̇*), their stress patterns being ——— + — and ——— + —, respectively. Similarly, the *G pl* forms вдов, строк, and зеркал (Nos. 8, 12, and 1) show stress on the stem when pronounced, yet only the first has true stem stress. This is because вдов is part of a pattern that has end stress in the singular and stem stress in the plural (*vdov+å*), and вдов would appear in ST as *vdóv+∅*. In the case of зеркал the reverse is true, with stress on the stem in the singular and on the

endings in the plural (ⱬ̆erkal+o). Thus the form зер-
ка́л would appear in ST as ⱬerkal+∅̸, since all forms of
the plural have end stress. The form стро́к is also
viewed as having stress on the zero ending (strok+∅̸),
but for a different reason; it is part of a pattern
(anomalous) in which there is stress on the stem in the
direct cases of the plural and on the endings in the
oblique cases (strok+à).

EXERCISE

Each of the twenty nouns on p. 21 has at least one form
with a zero ending (N sg or G pl). For each such form
decide whether the stress falls on the stem or on the
zero ending, and explain the basis for your decision.

3.   GENDER CONSTRAINTS

FIXED STRESS. Nouns of all three genders may
have fixed stress. The ——ˈ—— + — pattern is by far the
most numerous, containing over 30,000 nouns. The
—— + —ˈ— pattern is represented by approximately 2,200
nouns, most of which end in -∅. Among nouns that always
have fixed stress are: (1) those that have a N sg which
ends in unstressed -a (exceptions: дере́вня, до́ля);
and (2) most nouns with a derivational suffix that have
stress on this suffix in the N sg (e.g., грузови́к,
пятачо́к, купе́ц, моря́к, винцо́).

SHIFTING STRESS. Except for a few masculine
nouns with a N sg ending in -a (e.g., судья́, слуга́
старшина́), the —— + —ˣ variant of the shifting pattern is essentially nonmasculine. The only exceptions
to this among nouns ending in -∅ either contain some
irregularity in their declension or else exhibit a variant pattern of stress (fixed). In all, there are approximately 50 neuter and 100 feminine nouns with the
—— + —ˣ pattern. The ——ˣ—— + — variant of the shifting pattern is exclusively nonfeminine. It contains
the large (about 150) and growing group of masculine
nouns with a N pl ending in -á, a smaller group (about
80) of monosyllabic masculine nouns, and approximately
25 neuter nouns.

ANOMALOUS STRESS. This pattern is almost
exclusively nonneuter. (The only *regular* neuter nouns
with this pattern are крыльцо́ and тавро́.) The
⎯́⎯ + — variant contains about 50 masculine and 75
feminine nouns, all but two of which end in -∅ (до́ля
and дере́вня). The ⎯⎯ + ⎯̇ variant contains only 5
masculine nouns ending in -∅ and approximately 40 feminine nouns ending in -*a*.

THE *u*-RETRACTION. As already noted, this
subtype appears only among feminine nouns ending in -*â*,
of which about 13 have the shifting pattern and about
18 have the anomalous pattern.

D. EXCEPTIONS

The general rules regarding stress patterns which
have been outlined in this chapter admit almost no deviations, except in nouns that are in some other way irregular. Since such nouns will be treated elsewhere,[1]
their stress deviations need not be taken up at this
time. Thus only nouns that have a regular declensional
pattern will be included here.

1. The largest group of exceptions is made up of
approximately fifteen nouns in which stress is either on
the fill vowel when it is not expected to be, or not on
it when it should be. These nouns will be discussed in
Chapter 3 when the problem of the fill vowel is considered (see pp. 35-36).

2. The noun *ŏzor+o* has an unexpected shift not
to the endings in the plural, but to the other syllable
of the stem: озёра, озёра, озёр, озёрах, озё-
рам, озёрами.

3. The noun *xló̧pot+i* [*pl only*] has stress on the
second syllable of the stem in the *G pl*: хлопо́т.

_____

[1]See Chapter 9, especially Sec. F (pp. 141-44);
Item G,1,c,5) (pp. 146-47); Item G,3 (p. 149); and
Sec. I (p. 152).

4.   The noun $p\overset{x}{e}\underset{,}{r}od$+Ø has stress on the second syllable of the stem in the *N* and *A* *sg*: перёд, перёд, but переда, переде, переду, передом.

5.   In the noun $\underset{,}{t}agot$+$\overset{x}{a}$, the stress shifts back not *one* syllable, as is regular for this pattern, but to the first syllable of the stem in the plural: тя́готы, тя́готы, тя́гот, тя́готах, тя́готам, тя́готами.

6.   The nouns $d\underset{,}{e}\underset{,}{r}\grave{e}v/\underset{,}{n}$+$a$ and $stu\underset{,}{p}\grave{e}\underset{,}{n}$+Ø [*f*] are exceptions to the rule that in the anomalous pattern the stress alternates between the *first* syllable of the stem and the endings.

CHAPTER THREE

NOUN DECLENSION

The table below shows the endings in ST for all *regular* Russian nouns.

SINGULAR

Case	Nonfeminine		Nonneuter	Feminine
	MASC neut		fem som masc	
N	$-\emptyset$	$-o$	$-a$	$-\emptyset$
A			$-u$	
G	$-a$		$-i$	
P	$-e^1$		$-e^1$	$-i$
D	$-u$			
I	$-om$		$-oj(u)$	$-ju$

[1]Stems ending in ij- have $-i$ instead of $-e$.

PLURAL

Case	
N	$-i$ / $-a^2$
A	
G	$-\emptyset$ / $-ej$ / $-ov^2$
P	$-ax$
D	$-am$
I	$-ami$

[2]See Section A,4 on the plural for details regarding the distribution of these endings.

A. NOUN ENDINGS

When the basic principles of ST are applied, it
becomes possible to demonstrate that in the declension
of Russian nouns there is one set of endings for each
of the three major noun classes in the singular and
one set of endings for the plural. (See chart on preceding page.)

1. NONFEMININE DECLENSION. The declension of
neuter nouns is identical to that of masculine nouns in
-∅, except for the nominative and inanimate accusative
singular. (Since this declensional type contains no
feminine nouns, it will be designated the *nonfeminine*
declension.) In the nominative and inanimate accusative
singular the masculine nouns of this type have the ending -∅, i.e., no ending. This means that nothing is
added to the stem to form the nominative case of nouns
of this type. Neuter nouns have the ending -*o* in the
nominative and accusative singular, but all other forms
of the singular have the same endings as the masculine
nouns. If we examine a few nouns of this type we can
see that the stem of such nouns (indeed of *every* noun)
ends in a consonant to which are added endings that
generally begin with a vowel. (The only exceptions are
the zero ending and the ending -*ju*.) The rules relating
to the combination of consonants and vowels, discussed
in Chapter 1, are thus of primary importance here. As
examples let us consider the following nouns:

zavód+∅	ok/n+ŏ
vólk+∅	pól̦+o
p̦isáțel̦+∅	zdán̦ij+o
saráj+∅	b̦el̦j+ó
nož+∅	șĕrd/c+o

If we refer to the table of endings we will note
that the ending -∅ for masculines will be spelled with a
consonant letter either followed by nothing (завóд,
вóлк, сарáй, нóж) or by a soft sign (писáтель).
The soft sign here is used to indicate a soft paired
consonant not followed by a vowel. In the case of the

neuter nouns the ending -*o* may be spelled with the letter о (окнó), ё (бельё), or е (пóле, здáние,
сéрдце), depending on the stress and the nature of the
consonant preceding the -*o*.

In adding the ending -*a* to the stem of these nouns
to form the genitive case, we again must pay attention
to the nature of the consonant preceding this ending.
If the consonant is a hard paired consonant, a velar, a
husher, or *c*, then the combination with -*a* will be written with a vowel letter from Group I: завóда, окнá,
вóлка, ножá, сéрдца. However, when the preceding
consonant is a soft paired one or *j*, then this combination must be written with a vowel letter from Group II:
писáтеля, пóля, сарáя, здáния, бельá.

The spelling of the dative case ending -*u* follows
the same pattern as that of the ending -*a*, with the
Group I vowel used after a hard paired consonant, a
velar, a husher, or *c* (завóду, окнý, вóлку, ножý,
сéрдцу), and the corresponding Group II vowel after
a soft paired consonant or *j* (писáтелю, пóлю, са-
рáю, здáнию, бельý).

In spelling the instrumental case ending -*om*,
attention must again be focused both on the position
of the stress as well as on the nature of the preceding
consonant. Thus, завóдом, окнóм, вóлком, ножóм,
but сéрдцем, писáтелем, пóлем, сарáем, бельём.

Note that the prepositional case ending -*e* is
spelled only with a Group II letter, since before this
vowel a preceding paired consonant is always soft, and
the combination of any unpaired consonant with -*e* is
written with a vowel letter from Group II. Note, too,
that when the stem of the noun ends in *ij*- the ending -*e*
is replaced by -*i*. Thus, завóде, окнé, вóлке, но-
жé, сéрдце, писáтеле, пóле, сарáе, бельé, but
здáнии.

2. NONNEUTER DECLENSION. When we turn to the
second class of nouns, those with the ending -*a* in the
nominative singular, we find a similar situation. (This
group of nouns will be designated *nonneuter*, since it
contains no neuter nouns.) As examples let us take the
following nouns:

        mám+a   devíc+a

        kníg+a   grúš+a

ba̓n̦+a   all̦éj+a

istóṛij+a   staṭ/j+a̓

The spelling of the nominative case involves the
same rules as the genitive case of the nonfeminine
class, since in both instances we are dealing with the
ending -*a*. Thus after a hard paired consonant, a velar, a husher, or *c*, we find the Group I vowel letter
(ма́ма, кни́га, гру́ша, деви́ца), while after a soft
paired consonant or *j* the Group II vowel letter must be
used (ба́ня, алле́я, исто́рия, статья́). The accusative ending -*u* involves the same rules noted for the
dative case of the nonfeminine class, since the vowel
is the same in both instances: ма́му, кни́гу, гру́шу,
деви́цу, but ба́ню, исто́рию, алле́ю, статью́. The
ending of the genitive case (-*i*) provides examples of
combinations not yet discussed. Remember that before -*i*
velars are automatically soft and that the combination
of soft paired consonants, hushers, or *j* with -*i* is always written with a vowel letter from Group II. Therefore, only in two instances (i.e., when a hard paired
consonant or *c* combines with -*i*) do we find the vowel
letter from Group I (ма́мы, деви́цы). All of the other
examples will have the corresponding vowel letter from
Group II, either because of the combination of the vowel
-*i* with a soft paired consonant (ба́ни), a velar (кни́-
ги), a husher (гру́ши), or *j* (алле́и, исто́рии,
статьи́). Since the instrumental ending -*oj* begins
with the vowel *o*, the same rules noted above for -*o*
and -*om* apply here as well. Thus: ма́мой, кни́гой,
but деви́цей, гру́шей, ба́ней, исто́рией, алле́ей,
and статьёй. The ending -*e* has been treated above,
and the results are similar here: ма́ме, кни́ге, де-
ви́це, гру́ше, ба́не, алле́е, статье́, but исто́рии.

3. FEMININE DECLENSION. The third class of nouns
is the only one that contains nouns of only one gender
(feminine), and can be referred to by that designation.
Nouns of this third class have a nominative singular in
-∅, and the stems of these nouns always end in either a
soft paired consonant or a husher. If the rules regarding the use of the soft sign are recalled (B,1,b, p. 10;
B,2,c, p. 11), it will be seen that the nominative and
accusative singular of all nouns of this type will be
written with a soft sign for one of two reasons: (1) if

the stem ends in a soft paired consonant (e.g., $dv\grave{e}r+\emptyset$),
then the soft sign is necessary to indicate a soft
paired consonant not followed by a vowel; or (2) if the
stem ends in a husher, then the soft sign is written as
an orthographical convention (e.g., вéщь).

Similarly, the ending $-i$ for the genitive, prepositional, and dative case of nouns in this class will
always be written with a vowel letter from Group II,
because this vowel is always preceded by a soft paired
consonant or a husher (двéри, вéщи). The instru-
mental case ending $-ju$, the only ending (other than $-\emptyset$)
which does not begin with a vowel, will always involve
a soft sign, since all stems end in a consonant, and the
combination of consonant with j is written in Russian
with a soft sign (except at the boundary between prefix
and root). Thus: двéрью and вéщью from $dv\grave{e}r+ju$
and $v\grave{e}\check{s}\check{c}+ju$. (See Chapter 1, Section C,2.)

4. PLURAL. There are two endings for the nominative and inanimate accusative plural of all *regular*
Russian nouns: $-i$ and $-a$. The ending $-a$ is for all
neuter nouns and a small but growing number of masculine
nouns. Since this ending is exceptional for masculine
nouns, it must always be noted in the base form, and
such nouns will be indicated by means of the letter a
in square brackets, e.g., $g\grave{o}rod+\emptyset$ [a]. (In all but two
nouns, $rukav+\emptyset$ and $ob\check{s}lag+\emptyset$, the stress pattern $\overline{\underset{}{}\overset{x}{}} + -$
is seen to predominate for nouns of this type.) All
other regular nouns (i.e., all feminines and the remaining masculines) have the ending $-i$ in this case.

The genitive case may have any one of three possible endings distributed as follows:

If base form ends in	then G pl ending is
a vowel,	$-\emptyset$;
$-\emptyset$ preceded by a soft paired conso- nant or a husher,	$-ej$;
$-\emptyset$ preceded by anything else (i.e., a hard paired conso- nant, a velar, c, or j),	$-ov$.

It should be noted that here, as elsewhere, it is
necessary to keep the basic spelling rules in mind,
i.e., that the ending -i may be spelled either ы or и
depending on the preceding consonant; that -a may be
spelled а or я in dependence on the same considera-
tions; that the ending -ov may be spelled ов, ёв, or
ев depending on the nature of the preceding consonant
and the place of stress; and that the spelling of the
ending -$\emptyset$ will be subject to the basic spelling rules
regarding consonants not followed by a vowel. The
spelling of the prepositional, dative and instrumental
endings -ax,-am, and -$am̧i$, since all three begin with a,
creates no difficulties as long as the same basic
spelling rules are recalled, and these endings will be
spelled either ах, ам, ами or ях, ям, ями, in
dependence upon the nature of the preceding consonant.

EXAMPLES

Base form	N pl	G pl	D pl
kómnat+a	kómnat+i (кóмнаты)	kómnat+∅ (кóмнат)	kómnat+am (кóмнатам)
kņíg+a	kņíg+i (кнíги)	kņíg+∅ (кнíг)	kņíg+am (кнíгам)
grúš+a	grúš+i (грýши)	grúš+∅ (грýш)	grúš+am (грýшам)
blox+à	blóx+i (блóхи)	blox+∅́ (блóх)	blox+ám (блохáм)
ņeḑéḷ+a	ņeḑéḷ+i (недéли)	ņeḑéḷ+∅ (недéль)	ņeḑéḷ+am (недéлям)
istóŗij+a	istóŗij+i (истóрии)	istóŗij+∅ (истóрий)	istóŗij+am (истóриям)
ḑěl+o	ḑel+á (делá)	ḑel+∅́ (дéл)	ḑel+ám (делáм)
v̧in+ǒ	v̧ín+a (вíна)	v̧ín+∅ (вíн)	v̧ín+am (вíнам)

zdán̢ij+o   zdán̢ij+a   zdán̢ij+∅   zdán̢ij+am
              (здáния)   (здáний)   (здáниям)

dvér̢+∅ [f]   dvér̢+i   dver̢+éj   dver̢+ám
              (двéри)   (дверéй)   (дверя́м)

kon̢+∅̌   kón̢+i   kon̢+éj   kon̢+ám
              (кóни)   (конéй)   (коня́м)

plašč+∅̇   plašč+í   plašč+éj   plašč+ám
              (плащи́)   (плащéй)   (плаща́м)

nòč+∅ [f]   nóč+i   noč+éj   noč+ám
              (нóчи)   (ночéй)   (ноча́м)

učĭt̢el̢+∅ [a] učit̢el̢+á   učit̢el̢+éj   učit̢el̢+ám
              (учителя́)   (учителéй)   (учителя́м)

zavȯd+∅   zavód+i   zavód+ov   zavód+am
              (завóды)   (завóдов)   (завóдам)

vòlk+∅   vólk+i   volk+óv   volk+ám
              (вóлки)   (волкóв)   (волка́м)

m̢ésạac+∅   m̢ésạac+i   m̢ésạac+ov   m̢ésạac+am
              (мéсяцы)   (мéсяцев)   (мéсяцам)

gén̢ij+∅   gén̢ij+i   gén̢ij+ov   gén̢ij+am
              (гéнии)   (гéниев)   (гéниям)

bòj+∅   boj+í   boj+óv   boj+ám
              (бой)   (боёв)   (боя́м)

EXERCISE

For each of the examples above be prepared to explain:

1) the choice of ending in the *N pl* and *G pl*;
2) the spelling of the three plural forms given;
3) the position of the stress in each plural form.

B. THE FILL VOWEL

In declension whenever a nonvocalic ending (i.e.,
an ending that does not begin with a vowel) is added to
a stem that ends in more than one consonant, a fill
vowel *may* appear between the two final consonants of
the stem. The key word in the above statement is *may*,
since a fill vowel will not appear in all such instances. This will not present a problem for our analysis of declension, since the base form will always indicate, by means of a slash (e.g., *sos/n+ǎ*, but *voln+à*),
whether or not there will be a fill vowel in the form
with a nonvocalic ending. Note that there are only two
such endings in noun declension, the endings *-Ø* and *-ju*,
and that the stress in such forms can never be pronounced on that ending, even though technically it may
be said to fall there. (See Chapter 2, Section C,2.)

The three basic vowel units which may appear as
the fill vowel are *o*, *e*, and *i*. Before *e* and *i* a paired
consonant will *always* soften; before *o* it *generally*
does, except when *k* is the final consonant of the cluster, or in a stem with a nonsyllabic root (i.e., one
that does not contain a vowel) ending in a hard consonant. The fill vowel is normally *o*, except that it is
replaced by: (1) *e* after nonvelar consonants and before
any soft consonant or *c*; or (2) *i* before the consonant *j*
when stress does not fall on the fill vowel. Note that
the position of the stress in any form in which a fill
vowel is inserted should be determined *before* inserting
the vowel. For example, to generate the *G pl* of the
noun *sos/n+ǎ*, first position the stress (*sós/n+Ø*), then
insert the fill vowel (*sóson+Ø*), giving сóсен. If that
sequence were not followed, the result would be *сосён.

EXAMPLES

Base form	Form with fill vowel (*N sg* or *G pl*)	
sos/n+ǎ	sóson+Ø	сóсен
or/l+Ǿ	oról+Ǿ	орёл
vod/r+ǒ	vódor+Ø	вёдер

čis/l+ŏ	číşol+∅	чи́сел
kočer/g+à	kočeŗog+∅	кочерёг
țuŗ/m+ă̆	țúŗom+∅	тю́рем
kņaž/n+à	kņažon+∅́	княжо́н
rúč/k+a	rúčok+∅	ру́чек
koŗ́ej/k+a	koŗ́ejok+∅	копе́ек
dos/k+à [←]	dosok+∅́	досо́к
ok/n+ŏ	ókon+∅	о́кон
r/t+∅́	rot+∅́	ро́т
og/ņ+∅́	ogoņ+∅́	ого́нь
şĕrd/c+o	şeŗqec+∅́	серде́ц
ruč/j+∅́	ručej+∅́	руче́й
soloγ/j+∅́	soloγej+∅́	соловѐй
kàm/ņ+∅	kámeņ+∅	ка́мень
ot/c+∅́	oțec+∅́	отѐц
gósț/j+a	gósțij+∅	го́стий
lgúņ/j+a	lgúņij+∅	лгу́ний
poγéŗ/j+o	poγéŗij+∅	пове́рий

EXERCISE

For each of the examples above be prepared to explain:

1) the choice of fill vowel (i.e., vowel unit);
2) the choice of vowel letter;
3) the position of the stress.

EXCEPTIONS

There are two major types of deviation affecting the fill vowel. The first concerns the place of stress, the second, the nature of the fill vowel itself.

1. In a small group of nouns we find stress either on the fill vowel when it is not expected to be, or not on it when it should be. To the former group belong:

ẕem/ḽ+ǎ [←]	земе́ль
ov/c+ǎ	ове́ц
sv̧iṇ/j+ǎ	свине́й
şeṃ/j+ǎ	семе́й
suḓ/j+ǎ [m]	суде́й
şost/r+ǎ	сестёр
koḽ/c+ǒ	коле́ц
za̍j/m+∅	заём
na̍j/m+∅	наём
jaj/c+ǒ	яи́ц

Note that in the last noun above, in addition to the stress deviation the fill vowel is *i* instead of the expected *e* (i.e., *jajíc+∅*).

A smaller group of nouns has stress not on the fill vowel when it is expected to be:

ug/l+∅̍	у́гол
ug/ṛ+∅̍	у́горь
uz/l+∅̍	у́зел
ug/ḽ+∅̍	у́голь

mǎs/l+o   ма́сел

d̦è ̦ŋ/g+i [*Pl* only]   де́нег

All of these nouns may be indicated by means of a
slash enclosed in square brackets [/] following the base
form. The meaning of this symbol will be: stress not
on the expected syllable in any form with a nonvocalic
ending. For example, in the base form *ov/c+ǎ* [/], if
the [/] were not there, the expected form of the *G pl*
would be *о́вец, instead of the correct ове́ц.

2. The following nouns have either an unpredictable choice of fill vowel, unexpected softening, or the
absence of expected softening before the fill vowel:

a.   The noun *zá ̣j/c+∅* has *a* instead of *e*:   за́яц.

b.   The nouns *ruž/j+ŏ̌*, *ú ̣l/j+∅*, and *či ̣r̦/j+∅* have
e instead of *i*:   ру́жей, у́лей, чи́рей.

c.   The noun *l̦/v+∅̸* has *e* instead of *o*:   лёв.

d.   The noun *p/s+∅̸*, although nonsyllabic, has
softening of the consonant preceding the fill vowel *o*:
пёс.

e.   The noun *l̦ub/v̦+∅̸* [*f; Sg only*] has *o* instead
of *e* and no softening of the preceding consonant: лю-
бо́вь, любо́вью.

C.   THE BASE FORM

It should now be clear that the base form of a
noun is a device, an abstract notion, the main function
of which is to provide the student with all of the information needed about a given noun, in order to be
able to generate all of the declensional forms of that
noun with their proper stresses. The base form will
most closely resemble the nominative singular of the
given noun, but will contain other information regarding the gender, stress pattern, presence of a fill vowel
in a form with a nonvocalic ending, or about any unpredictable elements in the declension of that noun. We
have already seen that one of the three stress symbols

will always be present in the base form. A plus sign is
used to indicate the separation of stem from ending, a
slash to signify that a fill vowel will appear in any
form with a nonvocalic ending. The gender of most nouns
can be determined simply by looking at the ending (-∅
for masculine, -o for neuter, -a for feminine); deviations from this pattern must be noted. Thus, feminine
nouns ending in -∅ will be indicated by [f], and masculines ending in -a by [m]. For example, *nòč+∅* [f] or
slug+ă [m]. The notation [a] is used to cite those
masculine nouns that have the ending -a instead of the
expected -i in the nominative plural. Nouns marked with
[←] are those feminine nouns ending in -â with a shift
of stress to the stem in the accusative singular (i.e.,
nouns with the *u*-retraction). Finally, as we have just
seen, the symbol [/] will be used to indicate those
nouns in which stress in forms with a nonvocalic ending
is not on the expected syllable.

EXERCISES

        1.   What information is provided by each of the
base forms listed below?

        2.   Be prepared to decline each of the nouns
represented by the base forms listed below.

        1.   ădr̦es+∅ [a]   9.   v̦os/n+ă

        2.   árm̦ij+a   10.   vrač+∅́

        3.   bábuš/k+a   11.   v/š+∅́ [f]

        4.   bòg+∅   12.   gerój+∅

        5.   bol̦ézn̦+∅ [f]   13.   gor+à [←]

        6.   bol̦n̦íc+a   14.   gòsț+∅

        7.   vístav/k+a   15.   grùd̦+∅ [f]

        8.   vod+ằ [←]   16.   dv̦èr̦+∅ [f]

17. ḍevčón/k+a   39. nož+ǿ

18. ḍěl+o   40. ok/n+ŏ

19. d/ņ+ǿ   41. ot/c+ǿ

20. dožḍ+ǿ   42. pàr/ņ+ø

21. dolot+ŏ   43. ṛirož/k+ǿ

22. duš+ǎ [←]   44. poṛád/k+ø

23. zaņáṭij+o   45. ṛat/n+ŏ

24. zvon/k+ǿ   46. rín/k+ø

25. zdáņij+o   47. rubḷ+ǿ

26. ẕem/ḷ+ǎ [←][/]   48. ṣeṛ/g+à

27. zùb+ø   49. ṣěrd/c+o

28. kon/c+ǿ   ●50. ṣol+ŏ

29. koṛéj/k+a   51. ṣost/r+ǎ [/]

30. kòsṭ+ø [f]   52. sṛed+à [←]

31. ḷékcij+a   53. stǎd+o

32. ḷic+ŏ   54. staršin+ǎ [m]

33. lòšaḍ+ø [f]   55. suḍ/j+ǎ [m][/]

34. mǎsṭer+ø [a]   56. tòč/k+a

35. ṃéṣac+ø   57. učǐṭeḷ+ø [a]

36. molod/c+ǿ   58. čis/l+ŏ

37. ņeḍéḷ+a   59. šút/k+a

38. ņém/c+ø   60. jǎkoṛ+ø [a]

EXERCISE

For each of the *hypothetical* nouns listed below, you are to write *in Cyrillic* with its proper stress on each form the *N sg*, *G sg*, *I sg*, *N pl*, *G pl*, and *D pl*.

1. bar̨/j+ŏ   9. sul̨/j+ǎ [/]

2. zobár+∅   10. pŏkar̨+∅ [a]

3. trál/k+a   11. porot+à [←]

4. mus/n+ǎ [←]   12. n̨ič/j+∅́

5. bùr/n̨+∅   13. vět/r+o

6. t̨od/r+ŏ   14. tòl̨+∅ [f]

7. l/t+∅́   15. dob/r+à

8. rozd̨+∅́

Give the *A sg* of Nos. 3, 4, 9, 11, and 15.

QUESTIONS FOR THOUGHT AND DISCUSSION

1. The base form provides all of the information necessary to enable you to generate all of the forms of any given noun. How is this information usually supplied in a dictionary or other reference work?

2. Why is the nominative singular form alone inadequate for this purpose?

3. Are there ever any instances when the nominative singular form does provide adequate information? Explain.

4. In the exercise on p. 21 you were given six case forms for each noun and were asked to identify the stress pattern of these nouns. In no instance did you need all six forms. Which forms of each noun could have been omitted? Explain.

EXERCISE

Provide a base form for the following nouns:

	N sg	A sg	G sg	N pl	G pl	D pl
1.	кошелёк	кошелёк	кошелькá	кошелькú	кошелькóв	кошелькáм
2.	спинá	спúну	спинú	спúны	спúн	спинáм
3.	бедрó	бедрó	бедрá	бёдра	бёдер	бёдрам
4.	статья́	статью́	статьú	статьú	статéй	статья́м
5.	купéц	купцá	купцá	купцú	купцóв	купцáм
6.	кольцó	кольцó	кольцá	кóльца	колéц	кóльцам
7.	пóвесть	пóвесть	пóвести	пóвести	повестéй	повестя́м
8.	головá	гóлову	головы́	гóловы	голóв	головáм
9.	огóнь	огóнь	огня́	огнú	огнéй	огня́м
10.	щекá	щёку	щекú	щёки	щёк	щекáм
11.	вéк	вéк	вéка	векá	векóв	векáм
12.	ковёр	ковёр	коврá	коврú	коврóв	коврáм
13.	червь	червя́	червя́	чéрви	червéй	червя́м
14.	слезá	слезу́	слезú	слёзы	слёз	слезáм
15.	крыльцó	крыльцó	крыльцá	крыльца	крылéц	крыльцáм
16.	ручéй	ручéй	ручья́	ручьú	ручьёв	ручья́м
17.	полосá	полосу́	полосы́	пóлосы	полóс	полосáм
18.	круг	круг	кругá	кругú	кругóв	кругáм
19.	губá	губу́	губы́	гу́бы	гу́б	губáм
20.	стéбель	стéбель	стéбля	стéбли	стеблéй	стебля́м

+a

košel'/k+a
spin+a
bed/r+o
stat'/j+a
kupec+∅
kól'c+o
povest'+∅
golov+a

	N sg	A sg	G sg	N pl	G pl	D pl
21.	лоб	лоб	лба	лбы	лбов	лбам
22.	ла́герь	ла́герь	ла́геря	лагеря́	лагере́й	лагеря́м
23.	сва́тья	сва́тью	сва́тьи	сва́тьи	сва́тий	сва́тьям
24.	стекло́	стекло́	стекла́	стёкла	стёкол	стёклам
25.	война́	войну́	войны́	во́йны	войн	во́йнам
26.	разбо́й	разбо́й	разбо́я	разбо́и	разбо́ев	разбо́ям
27.	латви́йка	латви́йку	латви́йки	латви́йки	латви́ек	латви́йкам
28.	река́	ре́ку	реки́	ре́ки	рек	река́м
29.	груздь	груздь	груздя́	гру́зди	грузде́й	груздя́м
30.	верста́	версту́	версты́	вёрсты	вёрст	вёрстам
31.	седло́	седло́	седла́	сёдла	сёдел	сёдлам
32.	зима́	зи́му	зимы́	зи́мы	зим	зи́мам
33.	ло́коть	ло́коть	ло́ктя	ло́кти	локте́й	локтя́м
34.	колея́	колею́	колеи́	колеи́	коле́й	коле́ям
35.	ядро́	ядро́	ядра́	я́дра	я́дер	я́драм
36.	фона́рь	фона́рь	фонаря́	фонари́	фонаре́й	фонаря́м
37.	боги́ня	боги́ню	боги́ни	боги́ни	боги́нь	боги́ням
38.	о́бласть	о́бласть	о́бласти	о́бласти	областе́й	областя́м
39.	колесо́	колесо́	колеса́	колёса	колёс	колёсам
40.	высота́	высоту́	высоты́	высо́ты	высо́т	высо́там
41.	змея́	змею́	змеи́	зме́и	змей	зме́ям
42.	котёл	котёл	котла́	котлы́	котло́в	котла́м
43.	письмо́	письмо́	письма́	пи́сьма	пи́сем	пи́сьмам

Sc+φ

	N sg	A sg	G sg	N pl	G pl	D pl
44.	кочергá	кочергý	кочергú	кочергú	кочерёг	кочергáм
45.	гóлубь	гóлубя	гóлубя	гóлуби	голубéй	голубя́м
46.	тéло	тéло	тéла	телá	тéл	телáм
47.	корáбль	короля́	короля́	королú	королéй	короля́м
48.	стóрож	стóрожа	стóрожа	сторожá	сторожéй	сторожáм
49.	бревнó	бревнó	бревнá	брёвна	брёвен	брёвнам
50.	певýнья	певýнью	певýньи	певýньи	певýний	певýньям
51.	слóг	слóг	слóга	слóги	слогóв	слогáм
52.	платóк	платóк	платкá	платкú	платкóв	платкáм
53.	кáмень	кáмень	кáмня	кáмни	камнéй	камня́м
54.	бороздá	бороздý	бороздú	бóрозды	борóзд	бороздáм
55.	ногá	нóгу	ногú	нóги	нóг	ногáм
56.	скóрость	скóрость	скóрости	скóрости	скоростéй	скоростя́м
57.	гвóздь	гвóздь	гвоздя́	гвóзди	гвоздéй	гвоздя́м
58.	волокнó	волокнó	волокнá	волóкна	волóкон	волóкнам
59.	гáйка	гáйку	гáйки	гáйки	гáек	гáйкам
60.	тóполь	тóполь	тóполя	тополя́	тополéй	тополя́м
61.	нáция	нáцию	нáции	нáции	нáций	нáциям
62.	ребрó	ребрó	ребрá	рёбра	рёбер	рёбрам
63.	косá	кóсу	косú	кóсы	кóс	кóсам
64.	óчередь	óчередь	óчереди	óчереди	очередéй	очередя́м
65.	осёл	ослá	ослá	ослы́	ослóв	ослáм
66.	тропá	тропý	тропú	трóпы	трóп	тропáм

	N sg	A sg	G sg	N pl	G pl	D pl
67.	по́яс	по́яс	по́яса	пояса́	поясо́в	пояса́м
68.	лёд	лёд	льда́	льды́	льдо́в	льда́м
69.	простыня́	простыню́	простыни́	про́стыни	просты́нь	простыня́м
70.	сукно́	сукно́	сукна́	су́кна	су́кон	су́кнам
71.	блоха́	блоху́	блохи́	бло́хи	бло́х	блоха́м
72.	мешо́к	мешо́к	мешка́	мешки́	мешко́в	мешка́м
73.	метла́	метлу́	метлы́	мётлы	мётел	мётлам
74.	строй	строй	стро́я	строй	строёв	стро́ям
75.	конь	коня́	коня́	ко́ни	коне́й	коня́м
76.	княжна́	княжну́	княжны́	княжны́	княжо́н	княжна́м
77.	полотно́	полотно́	полотна́	поло́тна	поло́тен	полотнам
78.	ветвь	ветвь	ве́тви	ве́тви	ветве́й	ветвя́м
79.	скамья́	скамью́	скамьи́	скамьи́	скаме́й	скамья́м
80.	соловей	соловья́	соловья́	соловьи́	соловьёв	соловья́м
81.	тюрьма́	тюрьму́	тюрьмы́	тюрьмы́	тюрем	тюрьмам
82.	край	край	кра́я	края́	краёв	края́м
83.	царь	царя́	царя́	цари́	царе́й	царя́м
84.	колбаса́	колбасу́	колбасы́	колба́сы	колба́с	колба́сам
85.	ремесло́	ремесло́	ремесла́	ремёсла	ремёсел	ремёслам
86.	борода́	бо́роду	бороды́	бо́роды	боро́д	борода́м
87.	лебедь	лебедя	ле́бедя	ле́беди	лебеде́й	ле́бедям
88.	стройка	стро́йку	стро́йки	стро́йки	стро́ек	стро́йкам
89.	стена́	сте́ну	стены́	сте́ны	стен	стена́м
90.	серьга́	серьгу́	серьги́	се́рьги	серёг	серьга́м

EXERCISES

1. On the following page you are provided only
certain case forms of twenty-five nouns. For each noun
you should attempt to produce a base form. This will
not be possible in every instance, however, since for
some nouns you do not have sufficient information. You
should thus proceed in the following manner:

a. For which nouns are you able to produce a base
form? Do so.

b. For each of the remaining nouns state which
forms you need in order to produce a base form, and explain what information will be provided thereby.

c. Are there any forms given which you did not
need? Explain.

2. Below are listed ten *hypothetical* nouns in various cases. For each form you should be ready to answer
two questions:

a. What case (or cases) might each form be?

b. Produce a base form for each answer in *a*,
above.

1.	сучéй	6.	пýку
2.	тýглы	7.	бужбй
3.	глáм	8.	пеклá
4.	дбне	9.	блажбк
5.	брбв	10.	глбдью

	N sg	A sg	G sg	N pl	G pl	D pl
1.	бок	—	бо́ка	бока́	—	—
2.	борона́	бо́рону	—	—	—	—
3.	—	—	ве́тра	ве́тры	—	ветра́м
4.	гость	—	—	го́сти	гостéй	—
5.	—	дро́гу	—	дро́ги	дро́г	дро́гам
6.	душа́	ду́шу	—	—	—	—
7.	железа́	железу́	—	же́лезы	—	—
8.	—	кирку́	—	—	ки́рок	—
9.	копна́	копну́	—	—	копён	копна́м
10.	королёва	—	—	—	—	—
11.	—	кро́ху	—	—	—	кроха́м
12.	кулёк	—	—	кулькѝ	—	—
13.	мозг	—	—	—	мозго́в	—
14.	—	—	мы́ши	мы́ши	мыше́й	—
15.	но́готь	—	но́гтя	—	ногте́й	ногтя́м
16.	—	—	о́строва	острова́	—	—
17.	плюсна́	—	—	—	плюсен	—
18.	—	по́ру	—	—	пор	пора́м
19.	пра́во	—	пра́ва	—	прав	—
20.	рядно́	—	—	—	ряден	—
21.	след	—	сле́да	—	следо́в	—
22.	—	слободу́	—	слободы	—	—
23.	сме́рть	—	—	—	смертéй	—
24.	соловей	соловья́	—	соловьѝ	—	—
25.	—	тошноту́	—	—	тошно́т	—

CHAPTER FOUR

ADJECTIVE DECLENSION

The table below shows the endings in ST for all Russian adjectives.

SINGULAR

Case	Masc	Neut	Feminine
N	$-ij$[1] ↕	$-ojo$	$-aja$
A			$-uju$
G	$-ogo$		$-oj$
P	$-om$		
D	$-omu$		
I	$-im$		

[1]When stressed this ending is $-oj$.

PLURAL

Case	
N	$-ije$ ↕
A	
G	$-ix$
P	
D	$-im$
I	$-imi$

A. DECLENSIONAL ENDINGS (LONG FORM)

As was the case with the declension of nouns,
there may be said to be one set of endings for *all*
Russian adjectives. The traditional division of adjective declension into three types (hard, soft, mixed)
can be shown to be unnecessarily complex when the rules
for combining basic units are applied.

1. STEMS ENDING IN A HARD PAIRED CONSONANT.
When the stem of an adjective ends in a hard paired
consonant, the combination of this consonant with any
of the four basic vowel units that occur as the first
element of an adjectival ending (*a, i, o, u*) is written with vowel letters from Group I (а, ы, о, у). Let
us take as examples of this type the two adjectives
глу́пый and молодо́й, the first an example of stem
stress, the second, of stress on the endings.

glúp+aja	глу́пая
glúp+ije	глу́пые
glúp+uju	глу́пую
glúp+omu	глу́пому

molod+ája	молода́я
molod+íje	молоды́е
molod+úju	молоду́ю
molod+ómu	молодо́му

2. STEMS ENDING IN A SOFT PAIRED CONSONANT.
The combination of a soft paired consonant with these
same four basic vowel units will obviously necessitate
the use of the corresponding vowel letters from Group II
(я, и, е, ю). Note that since there are no examples of
end stress among adjectives with a stem ending in a soft
paired consonant, the spelling of the basic vowel *o* will
always be rendered with the letter е, rather than ё.

şíņ+aja	си́няя
şíņ+ije	си́ние

 şíŋ+omu   синему

şíŋ+uju   синюю

3. STEMS ENDING IN ANYTHING ELSE. The group of
adjectives usually labeled *mixed* all have a stem which
ends in either a husher, a velar, or *c*. They are viewed
as a mixed group because sometimes the first letter of
their endings is written with a vowel letter from Group
I, while at other times it is written with a vowel letter from Group II. That is, to write the vowel units *a*
and *u*, only Group I letters are used; to write the
vowel unit *i* a Group I letter is used after *c*, while
after hushers and velars a Group II letter is used;
and the vowel unit *o*, it will be recalled, is written
with a Group I letter after velars regardless of the
stress, while after hushers or *c* its spelling is dependent upon the place of stress.
        As examples of this type let us take the ad-
jectives высо́кий, плохо́й, хоро́ший, большо́й, and
ку́цый, the first two ending in a velar, the next two in
a husher, and the last in *c*. An example of both stem
and end stress is provided for the velar and husher
stems; the small group of adjectives with a stem ending
in *c* always has stress fixed on the stem.

visók+aja	высо́кая	plox+ája	плоха́я
visók+ije	высо́кие	plox+íje	плохи́е
visók+omu	высо́кому	plox+ómu	плохо́му
visók+uju	высо́кую	plox+úju	плоху́ю
xoróš+aja	хоро́шая	boļš+ája	больша́я
xoróš+ije	хоро́шие	boļš+íje	больши́е
xoróš+omu	хоро́шему	boļš+ómu	большо́му
xoróš+uju	хоро́шую	boļš+úju	большу́ю

kúc+aja	ку́цая
kúc+ije	ку́цые
kúc+omu	ку́цему
kúc+uju	ку́цую

From the preceding it is apparent that as long as
the student keeps the basic spelling rules in mind,
this threefold division into hard, soft, and mixed
types can be ignored. As already noted, all endings
begin with one of the four basic vowel units a, i, o,
u, and the choice of which vowel letter to write will
depend, as was the case with noun endings, on the nature of the preceding consonant and, in the case of the
combination of hushers and c with o, on the position of
the stress as well.

B.   DECLENSIONAL ENDINGS (SHORT FORM)

In addition to the series of long form endings
outlined above, the overwhelming majority of qualita-
tive adjectives also possess a series of short forms.
These forms are used only in the predicate complement
and have the following endings:

masculine singular	$-\emptyset$
feminine singular	$-a$
neuter singular	$-o$
plural	$-i$

C.   ADJECTIVE STRESS

Stress in the long forms is always fixed either
on a syllable of the stem or on the first syllable of
the ending in all forms; it never shifts within the
paradigm as may occur in the noun. In the short forms,
however, shifting stress is often found and occurs in a
large number of very common adjectives. The pattern of
short form stress shift exhibits an opposition involving end stress in the feminine form and stress on the
stem in the other three forms. There may also be either
fixed stem stress or fixed end stress in the short

forms.   Examples of these types of short form stress
are:

fixed on stem	богáт, богáта, богáто, богáты
fixed on endings	хмелён, хмельнá, хмельнó, хмельнь́
shifting	грýб, грубá, грýбо, грýбы

D.   THE FILL VOWEL

The same rules noted for the fill vowel in nouns
(Chapter 3, Section B) also apply to the adjective, but
the situation is considerably simpler than in the noun
because the only vowel that appears in the adjective is
o.   For example:

Base form	Form with fill vowel	
jǎs/n+ij	jáz̦on+∅	ясен
čud/n+o̦j	čud̦on+∅́	чудён
g̦rěš/n+ij	g̦réšon+∅	грéшен
sm̦eš/n+o̦j	sm̦ešon+∅́	смешóн
tǒn/k+ij	tónok+∅	тóнок
gǒr̦/k+ij	gór̦ok+∅	гóрек
z/l+o̦j	zol+∅́	зол

Note the expected softening of the consonant preceding *o* in the first two examples and the spelling of *o*
following a husher in the next two examples where the
choice of vowel letter is determined by the stress.   In
the fifth example above, no softening occurs before *o*
because of the final *k*; in the sixth example the *r̦* is
already soft and remains so; in the seventh example no
softening occurs because the root is nonsyllabic.

EXCEPTIONS

1. No softening occurs in the adjectives
pŏl/n+ij and *dŏl/g+ij*, giving ПÓЛОН and ДÓЛОГ.

2. The fill vowel in the adjective *dostój/n+ij*
is *i* rather than the expected *o*, giving ДОСТÓИН (i.e.,
dostójin+∅).

E. THE BASE FORM

Adjectives that have only long forms need only
one symbol (') for their designation, since these adjectives have only fixed stress, either on the stem or
on the endings, in all forms of the paradigm. Adjectives that possess short forms may be divided into two
basic types: (1) those in which the stress of the
short form never shifts; and (2) those in which it
does. Each of these two basic types may be further
divided, depending on whether the stress in the long
forms is fixed on the stem or on the endings. There
are thus two variants of each of the two major patterns:

1.
    a) stress fixed on stem in long and
       short forms

    b) stress fixed on endings in long
       and short forms

2.
    a) stress fixed on stem in long forms,
       shifting in short forms

    b) stress fixed on endings in long forms,
       shifting in short forms

If we use the symbol (') to indicate those adjectives in which the stress never shifts (1,a and 1,b), we
may distinguish between them by placing the symbol in our
base form over the syllable of the stem that is stressed
in all forms, or by placing it over the ending. For
example, *bogát+ij* or *smeš/n+ój*.

Similarly, if we use the symbol (×) to indicate
those adjectives in which the stress of the short forms
exhibits the shifting pattern, we may at the same time

indicate the place of stress in the long forms by placing that symbol over either a syllable of the stem in
the base form or over the ending: *grắb+ij* (2,a) or
živ+ǒj (2,b).

There is, in addition, an anomalous type that has
stress fixed on the stem in the long forms, but on the
endings in the short forms. We can signal this pattern
by means of the symbol (ˋ), placing it over that syllable of the stem which is stressed in the long forms,
e.g., *goŗằč+ij*. Such a notation implies fixed stress
in all long forms on the syllable of the stem indicated
and stress on the endings in all short forms: (горя́ч,
горяча́, горячо́, горячи́й).

EXERCISES

1.   What information is provided by each of the
base forms listed below?

2.   Be prepared to give the long and short forms
of the adjectives represented by the base forms listed
below.

1.	grǒm/k+ij	6.	şed+ǒj
2.	xṃeḷ/n+òj	7.	žǎr/k+ij
3.	šǔm/n+ij	8.	udal+ǒj
4.	ţažòl+ij	9.	màl+ij
5.	xoròš+ij	10.	v̦ėč/n+ij

In addition to our three symbols, we will have to
make use of a few bracketed and parenthetical notations
in order to be able to provide complete information
about the stress of every adjective. The first of
these, [←], is used to indicate the stress pattern of
a small group of eight adjectives with a disyllabic
stem and shifting short form stress. In these adjectives the stress, though either on the second syllable
of the stem or on the endings in the long forms, retracts to the *first* syllable of the stem in the nonfeminine short forms. For example, in the adjective

u̯eg̊ŏl+ij [←] the stress falls on the second syllable in
all of the long forms (весёлый, весёлая, весёлое,
etc.), on the ending in the feminine short form (весе-
ла́), but on the first syllable of the stem in the other
short forms (ве́сел, ве́село, ве́селы). The other
adjectives belonging to this group are:

golŏd/n+ij [←]   dorog+ŏj [←]

d̦ošŏv+ij [←]   molod+ŏj [←]

z̦el̦ŏn+ij [←]   xolost+ŏj [←]

xolŏd/n+ij [←]

   The second additional notation, [/], involves the
place of stress in a form with a nonvocalic ending,
i.e., the zero ending of the masculine short form. In
about a dozen adjectives the stress in this form is
either on the fill vowel when it is not expected to be,
or not on it when it should be. (Compare a similar
situation in the noun, pp. 35-36.) In either instance
the deviation will be noted by [/] following the base
form. The basic meaning of this notation, as it was in
the noun, may be summarized as: stress not on the expected syllable in any form with a nonvocalic ending.
For example, in the adjectives l̦ŏg/k+ij [/], šŭst/r+ij
[/], if the [/] were not there, we would expect *лего́к
and *шу́стер, instead of the correct лёгок, шустёр.
   The final additional notation is one that is enclosed in parentheses and is used to signal not a deviation, as is the case with the bracketed symbols, but
rather that a form, or occasionally a whole pattern, exhibits permissible variation. For example, there are
about forty adjectives with shifting short form stress
in which the plural short form may have either the expected stem stress or may also have a variant with end
stress. Such adjectives may be noted as follows:
gŏrd+ij (p). The parenthetical notation provides the
information that the plural short form may be either
го́рды or горды́. Occasionally a masculine form will
exhibit variation, and this can be designated in a similar manner, e.g., smir̊/n+ij (m), implying either сми́-
рен or смирён. In other instances an adjective may
exhibit variation involving an entire pattern. Such
adjectives may be cited by placing the variant base

form in parentheses: *b̭ě̃l+ij (b̭ɛ̀l+ij)*. This notation
indicates that the long forms of both patterns have
stress fixed on the stem, but that the short forms may
either have shifting stress (бе́л, бела́, бе́ло, бе́лы)
or fixed end stress (бе́л, бела́, бело́, белы́). Only
about eleven adjectives exhibit this type of variation
(see below).

    Adjectives with the [←] deviation have already
been listed on the preceding page. The following adjectives belong to the anomalous group and are listed in
two subgroups. The first contains those adjectives
which have this pattern as their primary type; the second contains those adjectives that exhibit it as a variant of the shifting pattern.

SUBGROUP 1

gor̭ằč+ij   sv̭ɛ̀ž+ij (p)

daḽȯk+ij (daḽŏk+ij)   ṱȯm/n+ij [/] (ṱŏm/n+ij)

dȯlž/n+ij [/]   ṱažȯl+ij

ḽȯg/k+ij [/](p)   čȯr/n+ij [/] (čŏr/n+ij)

mà̀l+ij   xorȯš+ij

mudr̭ȯn+ij   širȯk+ij (širŏk+ij)

SUBGROUP 2

b̭ě̃l+ij (b̭ɛ̀l+ij)   r̭ŏstr+ij (r̭ȯstr+ij)

visŏk+ij (visȯk+ij)   pȯl/n+ij (pȯl/n+ij [/])

glubŏk+ij (glubȯk+ij)   stà̀r+ij (stà̀r+ij)

dḽĭn/n+ij (dḽìn/n+ij [/])   ṱŏp/l+ij (ṱȯp/l+ij [/])

žȯlt+ij (žȯlt+ij)   ŭm/n+ij [/] (ùm/n+ij)

m̭ŏrtv+ij (m̭ȯrtv+ij)

    Most of the adjectives with the [/] deviation be-
long to the anomalous pattern and have been listed in

one of the two subgroups above.   Only a few belong to
some other pattern.   They are:

bol̯/n+ój [/]   xĭt/r+ij [/]

ŭm/n+ij [/]   šŭst/r+ij [/]

F.   SPECIAL PROBLEMS

1.   The adjective короткий may have any one of
the following base forms: *korŏt/k+ij; korŏt/k+ij* [←];
korŏt/k+ij (n, p).

2.   When великий means 'great' it has the base
form *v̭el̯ĭk+ij*; when used for the short forms of боль-
шой, it has instead the base form *v̭el̯ĭk+ij (p).*

3.   When острый means 'sharp' in the literal
sense it has the base form *ŏstr+ij*; when it means 'wit-
ty' it has *òst/r+ij.*

4.   When здоровый means 'healthy' it has the
base form *zdoróv+ij*; when it means 'strong' it has the
base form *zdoròv+ij.*

5.   When вольный means 'free' it has the base
form *vòl̯/n+ij (p)*; when it means 'at liberty to' it has
vòl̯/n+ij [/].

6.   In the short forms of the adjective солёный
(base form: *sol̯ŏn+ij* [←]), the consonant l̯ hardens:
солон, солона, солоно, солоны.

7.   In the adjective счастливый, the stress of
the short forms is fixed either on the first syllable
or (optionally) on the second. If we understand the basic meaning of the symbol [←] to be "stress retracts to
the first syllable of the stem in those short forms
that have stress on the stem," then we can indicate the
pattern of this adjective as follows: *sčastl̯ív+ij* [←];
(sčastl̯ív+ij).

EXERCISES

    1. Write in Cyrillic with the correct stress mark the (1) *N sg masc*; (2) *N sg fem*; (3) *A sg fem*; (4) *D sg neut*; (5) *G pl*; (6) all short forms (including optional variants) of the adjectives represented by the base forms listed below.

1. h̬ěd/n+ij (p)

2. pr̬am+ǒj

3. krŭp/n+ij

4. v̬eč/n+ij

5. xǐt/r+ij [/]

6. bol̬/n+oj [/]

7. dal̬ȯk+ij (dal̬ǒk+ij)

8. xolost+ǒj [←]

9. dur/n+ǒj (p, m)

10. rȧv/n+ij [/]

11. čud/n+oj

12. udȯb/n+ij

13. xorȯš+ij

14. dr̬an/n+ǒj

15. m̬ǎg/k+ij

16. xolǒd/n+ij [←] (p)

17. sm̬ǐr/n+ij (m)

18. ŭm/n+ij [/] (ùm/n+ij)

19. d̬iv/n+ij

20. sv̬ẻž+ij (p)

21. p̬ȯstr+ij (p̬ȯstr+ij)

22. bl̬ǐz/k+ij (p)

23. t̬ǐx+ij

24. d̬ošȯv+ij [←]

25. sl̬ep+ǒj

26. t̬ȯp/l+ij (t̬ȯp/l+ij [/])

27. glubȯk+ij (glubȯk+ij)

28. gust+ǒj (p)

29. jȧv/n+ij

30. širȯk+ij (širȯk+ij)

31. mudr̬ȯn+ij

32. nag+ǒj

33. čǒr/n+ij [/] (čǒr/n+ij)

34. drŭž/n+ij (p)

35. strǎš/n+ij (p)

2. Provide a base form for the following adjectives:

N sg masc	short masc	short fem	short neut	short pl
1. смешнóй	смешóн	смешнá	смешнó	смешны́
2. бы́стрый	бы́стр	быстрá	бы́стро	бы́стры
3. немóй	нéм	немá	нéмо	нéмы
4. тяжёлый	тяжёл	тяжелá	тяжелó	тяжелы́
5. зелёный	зéлен	зеленá	зéлено	зéлены
6. тёмный	тёмен	темнá	темнó (тёмно)	темны́ (тёмны)
7. стóйкий	стóек	стойкá	стóйко	стóйки
8. лихóй	лих	лихá	лúхо	лúхи (лихи́)
9. жёлтый	жёлт	желтá	жёлто (желтó)	жёлты (желты́)
10. высóкий	высóк	высокá	высóко (высокó)	высóки (высокú)
11. дóлжный	дóлжен	должнá	должнó	должны́
12. рóвный	рóвен	ровнá	рóвно	рóвны
13. мáлый	мáл	малá	малó	малы́
14. ду́шный	ду́шен	душнá	ду́шно	ду́шны
15. сúльный	сúлен (силён)	сильнá	сúльно	сúльны (сильны́)

G.   SUMMARY OF ADJECTIVE STRESS

    1.   FIXED STRESS

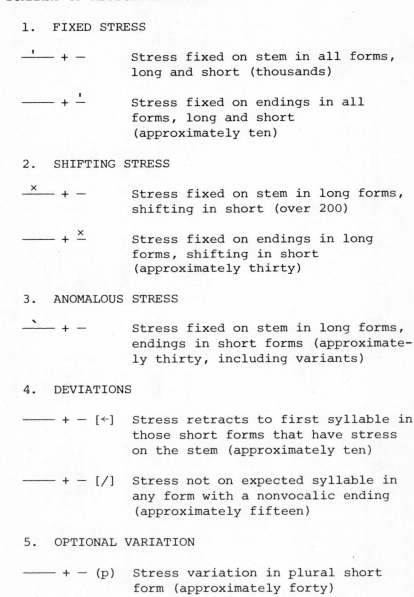

      ——́— + —   Stress fixed on stem in all forms,
                           long and short (thousands)

      —— + —́   Stress fixed on endings in all
                           forms, long and short
                           (approximately ten)

    2.   SHIFTING STRESS

      ——×— + —   Stress fixed on stem in long forms,
                           shifting in short (over 200)

      —— + —×   Stress fixed on endings in long
                           forms, shifting in short
                           (approximately thirty)

    3.   ANOMALOUS STRESS

      ——`— + —   Stress fixed on stem in long forms,
                           endings in short forms (approximate-
                           ly thirty, including variants)

    4.   DEVIATIONS

      —— + — [←]   Stress retracts to first syllable in
                           those short forms that have stress
                           on the stem (approximately ten)

      —— + — [/]   Stress not on expected syllable in
                            any form with a nonvocalic ending
                           (approximately fifteen)

    5.   OPTIONAL VARIATION

      —— + — (p)   Stress variation in plural short
                            form (approximately forty)

      (—— + —)   Stress variation affecting an
                            entire short form pattern
                           (approximately fifteen)

H. CONCLUSION

The same symbols have been used to designate patterns of stress in both the noun and the adjective,
and the basic meaning of these symbols may be said to
be identical, even though their specific implications
may vary. That is, in both the noun and the adjective
the symbol itself designates the basic pattern of
stress, while its position in the base form signals the
appropriate variant of that basic pattern. The symbol
(') carries a relatively uniform meaning: stress fixed
throughout the paradigm on that syllable over which the
symbol appears in the base form. The symbol for shifting stress (ˣ), though somewhat less uniform in its
specific implications, may be said to indicate the *basic* shifting pattern. In the noun it implies that the
place of stress of the singular is opposed to that of
the plural; in the adjective it signals an opposition
of feminine to nonfeminine short forms. In both the
noun and the adjective the position of the symbol informs us which variant of the basic shifting type will
occur: stem to endings or endings to stem in the noun,
fixed stem or end stress in the long forms of the adjective.

The symbol (ˋ) may be said to indicate a pattern
involving a shift of stress that diverges from the basic
shifting type. In the noun this implies a shift that
occurs within one of the numbers (plural), rather than
from one number to another; in the adjective it implies
an opposition between the place of stress in the long
forms and those of the short forms as a whole, rather
than between the feminine and nonfeminine short forms.
The symbol [←] designates a retraction of stress that
is not predictable from the basic symbol, in other words
a deviation within one of the basic patterns. It is
worth noting that in both the noun and the adjective
this symbol may be appended only to certain patterns,
i.e., to either ——— + $\overset{\times}{\underline{}}$ or ——— + $\overset{\backprime}{\underline{}}$ in the noun, and
to either $\overset{\times}{\underline{}}$ + — or ——— + $\overset{\times}{\underline{}}$ in the adjective. The
symbol [/] will always indicate, in either the noun or
the adjective, that in any form with a nonvocalic ending, stress will be either on the fill vowel when it is
not expected to be, or not on it when it should be.
Finally, notations enclosed in parentheses are used in
both the noun and the adjective to signal optional variation.

The division into fixed, shifting, anomalous, and deviational in that order not only grows naturally out of the data, but is supported by the fact that each pattern contains a larger number of examples than the next succeeding one. That is, the fixed pattern is by far the most numerous in both the noun and the adjective, the numbers in each instance running in the thousands. The shifting pattern is next, with approximately 400 for the noun and 250 for the adjective. The anomalous pattern is expectedly the least numerous of the three major types with approximately 170 for the noun and no more than 30 for the adjective. Only about 30 nouns and less than 10 adjectives exhibit the [←] retraction, and the number of nouns and adjectives with the [/] deviation is approximately 15 for each group. Stress variation appears to be more common in the adjective than in the noun, but in either instance it will be designated by means of a parenthetical, rather than bracketed, notation.

I.   A NOTE ON THE COMPARATIVE

A simple comparative, used only in the predicate, may be formed in Russian by adding to the stem of the adjective one of two formants (-*ee* or -*e*). The distribution of these formants is as follows:

1.   THE FORMANT -*ee*. Adjectives which have any suffix (except -*k*- or -*ok*-), as well as a few nonsuffixed adjectives, form a simple comparative by adding this formant. Stress will be on the first vowel of the formant whenever the ending is stressed in the feminine short form. Otherwise stress is fixed on the stem. For example:

но́вый	нове́е
сла́бый	слабе́е
тёплый	тепле́е
весёлый	веселе́е
холо́дный	холодне́е
краси́вый	краси́вее
си́льный	сильне́е
бе́дный	бедне́е

2.   THE FORMANT -*e*.   (Never stressed)

a.   The formant -*e* is added to the following
nonsuffixed adjectives. When this formant is added the
final consonant of the stem mutates.

густо́й	гу́ще
просто́й	про́ще
то́лстый	то́лще
ча́стый	ча́ще
чи́стый	чи́ще
ве́тхий	ве́тше
глухо́й	глу́ше
сухо́й	су́ше
ти́хий	ти́ше
дорого́й	доро́же
стро́гий	стро́же
туго́й	ту́же
отло́гий	отло́же
молодо́й	моло́же
твёрдый	тве́рже
бога́тый	бога́че
круто́й	кру́че
дешёвый	деше́вле

b.   The formant -*e* is added to the following
adjectives with the suffix -*k*- (or -*ok*-). Before the
formant is added the suffix drops, and the final consonant of the stem mutates.

га́дкий	га́же
гла́дкий	гла́же
жи́дкий	жи́же
ре́дкий	ре́же
бли́зкий	бли́же
ни́зкий	ни́же
у́зкий	у́же
коро́ткий	коро́че
высо́кий	вы́ше
широ́кий	ши́ре

c.   The formant -*e* is added to *all other* adjectives with the suffix -*k*-. Here the suffix does not
drop, but itself mutates to *č*. This group contains

slightly more than forty adjectives. Some common examples are:

гро́мкий	гро́мче
кре́пкий	кре́пче
лёгкий	ле́гче
ло́вкий	ло́вче
мя́гкий	мя́гче
ре́зкий	ре́зче
ро́бкий	ро́бче
я́ркий	я́рче

3. IRREGULARITIES. About a dozen adjectives form
simple comparatives irregularly, using the formants *-še*,
-že, or *-šče*. These formants are never stressed.

большо́й	бо́льше
ма́ленький	ме́ньше
ста́рый	ста́рше
далёкий	да́льше
до́лгий	до́льше
то́нкий	то́ньше
ра́нний	ра́ньше
хоро́ший	лу́чше
плохо́й	ху́же
по́здний	по́зже
глубо́кий	глу́бже
сла́дкий	сла́ще

Note the change of *o* to *e* in the adjectives дешё-
вый and лёгкий (дешёвле, ле́гче). For a similar
alternation in the verb, see Item 1, pp. 125-26.

CHAPTER FIVE

PRONOMINAL ADJECTIVE DECLENSION

The table below shows the endings in ST for all pronominal adjectives.

SINGULAR

Case	Masc	Neut	Feminine
N	$-\emptyset$	$-o$	$-a$
A	$\updownarrow$		$-u$
G	$-ogo$		
P	$-om$		$-oj$ [1]
D	$-omu$		
I	$-im$		

[1]After any soft consonant this ending becomes $-ej$.

PLURAL

Case	
N	$-i$
A	$\updownarrow$
G	$-ix$
P	
D	$-im$
I	$-imi$

A.   INTRODUCTION

As is clear from the table on the preceding page,
the declension of pronominal adjectives differs from
that of adjectives only in the endings of the direct
cases of the singular and plural.   In the direct case
forms the pronominal adjectives have endings that are
identical with noun endings (masculine, $-\emptyset$; neuter $-o$;
feminine, $-a$ and $-u$; plural, $-i$), while in the oblique
case forms the endings are identical with those of the
adjective declension.

There are two basic types of pronominal adjective,
suffixed and nonsuffixed.   To the first type belongs a
large number of possessive adjectives with one of three
suffixes ($-j-$, $-in-$, $-ov-$).   The second type contains
ten very common pronouns and the numeral один.

B.   THE SUFFIXED TYPE

1.   THE SUFFIX $-j-$.   This suffix is added to the
stem of certain nouns, usually nouns denoting animals
and, less commonly, humans.   When this suffix is added
certain changes are expected to occur in the stem of
the noun.   These changes may be summarized as follows:

    a.   The velars k, g, x mutate to $č$, $ž$, $š$.

        волк   волчий
        враг   вражий
        петух   петуший

    b.   The consonants d, t, c mutate to $ž$, $č$, $č$.

        верблюд   верблюжий
        цыплята   цыплячий
        птица   птичий

    c.   A fill vowel is regularly inserted in the
newly derived pronominal adjective stem if there is a
fill vowel on the declensional level in the original
noun.   For example, in the noun кошка $(ko\check{s}/k+a)$ the
genitive plural form (кошек) has a fill vowel because
of the nonvocalic ending ($-\emptyset$).   When $-j-$, a nonvocalic
suffix, is added to the stem $ko\check{s}/k+$ to derive a pronominal adjective, a fill vowel is likewise inserted and
becomes a permanent part of the new pronominal

adjective stem with the base form *kóšeč/j+*. Some other
examples are:

овца́ (ове́ц)   ове́чий
лягу́шка (лягу́шек)   лягу́шечий
куку́шка (куку́шек)   куку́шечий

    Since the suffix *-j-* is always added to a noun
stem, and since all stems end in a consonant, we are
dealing with the combination of consonant plus *j* everywhere except in the *N sg masc* (zero ending), where a
fill vowel appears between the two final consonants of
the stem. Note also that in the zero form the fill
vowel will always be *i*, since the consonant cluster
ends in *j*, and the stress is never on the fill vowel.
As examples let us take the pronominal adjectives
sobáč/j+ , formed from the noun *sobák+a*, and *barán/j+*
from the noun *barán+Ø*.

N sg masc	sobáčij+Ø (соба́чий)	baráṇij+Ø (бара́ний)
N sg neut	sobáčj+o (соба́чье)	baráṇj+o (бара́нье)
N sg fem	sobáčj+a (соба́чья)	baráṇj+a (бара́нья)
N plural	sobáčj+i (соба́чьи)	baráṇj+i (бара́ньи)
A sg fem	sobáčj+u (соба́чью)	baráṇj+u (бара́нью)
G sg masc	sobáčj+ogo (соба́чьего)	baráṇj+ogo (бара́ньего)
G sg fem	sobáčj+ej (соба́чьей)	baráṇj+ej (бара́ньей)

    With the exception of the *N sg masc* , every form
of the pronominal adjective with the suffix *-j-* will be
written with a consonant letter followed by a soft sign
plus one of the vowel letters from Group II. Since the
N sg masc will have the fill vowel *i* between some consonant and *j* followed by the zero ending, this form

will always be spelled with a consonant letter followed
by -ий. Unfortunately, this spelling often causes
students to confuse a pronominal adjective like соба́-
чий *(sobácij+∅)* or бара́ний *(baráņij+∅)* with an adjective like горя́чий *(goŗáč+ij)* or си́ний *(şíņ+ij)*,
since there is nothing in the *N sg masc* (i.e., the dictionary form usually used as the base form) to suggest
that they are not all declined in exactly the same way.
Once it is understood, however, that the pronominal adjectives of this type all have a stem ending in consonant plus *j* to which are added endings that everywhere
(except in the zero form) begin with a vowel, then the
difference between the two patterns can be seen. To
put it another way, any form other than the *N sg masc*
would clearly identify the declension as pronominal adjective rather than adjective type. For this reason,
it is unfortunate that the *N sg masc* is so often used
as the base form.

2. THE SUFFIX *-in-*. This suffix is added to the
stem of nouns denoting familial relationships or to the
stem of diminutives of Christian names. It is formed
primarily from nouns that have the ending *-a* in the *N
sg*. In the few instances when this suffix is added to
the stem of a noun that ends in *-∅* in the *N sg*, the
consonant *n* is inserted before the suffix. In either
case, a hard paired consonant will automatically soften
before the vowel *i* of this suffix. For example:

па́па	па́пин	Ма́ша	Ма́шин
ма́ма	ма́мин	О́ля	О́лин
ба́бушка	ба́бушкин	Та́ня	Та́нин
де́душка	де́душкин	Воло́дя	Воло́дин

It should also be added that in the syllable before the suffix a basic *o*, which follows a soft paired
consonant or a husher and precedes a hard paired consonant, regularly becomes *e* when that hard paired consonant softens before the suffix *-in-*. For example:

жена́ (žon+á)   же́нин
сестра́ (şostr+á)   се́стрин

If the final consonant of the stem is soft, however, the
o does not become *e*, e.g., тётя, тётин; тёща, тёщин.

3. THE SUFFIX -*ov*-. The suffix -*ov*-, much less
commonly used than -*in*-, is added to the stem of certain
nouns that have the ending -∅ in the *N sg* and denote
persons. For example:

старѝк   старикóв   цáрь   царёв
капитáн   капитáнов   отéц   отцóв
                           (отц-)

4. STRESS. Stress in the suffixed pronominal
adjectives may *never* be on the endings and is always
fixed on the same syllable in all forms of the paradigm. In the -*ov*- type, stress generally falls on the
same syllable that bears the stress in the *N sg* of the
noun from which it is derived. Therefore, a pronominal
adjective of this type, derived from a noun with stress
on the ending in the *N sg*, will have stress on the *o* of
the suffix, e.g., старѝк, старикóв.
    In both the -*j*- and -*in*- types stress will always
fall either on the syllable directly preceding the suffix or on an earlier syllable, if that syllable is
stressed in the *N sg* of the noun from which the pronominal adjective is derived. The only exceptions to this
are the three pronominal adjectives снохѝн, княжнѝн,
сатанѝн (from снохá, княжнá, сатанá) with stress
on the suffix.

5. GENERAL COMMENTS. Of the three types of suffixed pronominal adjectives, only the -*j*- type is ac-
corded full literary status. The -*in*- and -*ov*- types
are not generally found in scholarly or publicistic
prose, but in colloquial or conversational Russian the
forms with the suffix -*in*- are widely used. Forms with
the suffix -*ov*-, on the other hand, are very rare, even
in colloquial Russian.
    In the declension of pronominal adjectives with
the suffix -*in*- or -*ov*- alternate forms of the *G* and *D*
sg masc/neut are occasionally found with noun endings,
rather than adjectival ones (пáпина, пáпину for пá-
пиного, пáпиному). Such forms, once standard, are
more and more giving way to the longer, adjectival
forms, which are now regularly sanctioned by most
authorities.

EXERCISES

1. Explain the formation of the following pronominal adjectives. (That is, identify the noun from which each one is derived, and explain any changes in its stem that have occurred in forming the pronominal adjective.) The *N sg fem* is provided as the dictionary form.

1.	челове́чья *челове́к*	**19.**	белу́жья *белуга*
2.	ребя́чья *ребя́тка*	20.	дя́дина *дядя*
3.	стару́шья *старука*	21.	вну́чья *внук*
4.	ня́нина	22.	вдо́вья *вдова*
5.	А́ннушкина	23.	золо́вкина
6.	шака́лья *шака́л*	24.	Ка́тина
7.	деви́чья *девица*	25.	медве́жья *медвед*
8.	лягу́шечья *лягушка*	26.	ра́бья *раб*
9.	оле́нья *оле́нь*	27.	ко́зья *коза*
10.	неве́сткина	28.	охо́тничья *охотник*
11.	Са́шенькина	29.	стару́шечья *старушка*
12.	коро́вья *корова*	30.	каза́чья *казак*
13.	пасту́шья *пастух*	31.	мы́шья *мышь мышь*
14.	Серёжина *дочерний*	32.	суда́чья *судак*
15.	доче́рнина *дочернина*	33.	бы́чья *бычок бок*
16.	отцо́ва *отец*	34.	бо́жья *бог*
17.	ли́сья *лиса*	35.	лиси́чья *лисица*
18.	ку́рья *куры*		

šakal -/j+a (6.)
olen' -/j+a (9.)
know 35
there
pAstux -/j+1 (13.)

2. Be prepared to give the following case forms for each of the pronominal adjectives above:

a.	*N sg masc*	f.	*D sg neut*
b.	*N sg neut*	g.	*I sg masc*
c.	*A sg fem*	h.	*D sg fem*
d.	*N plural*	i.	*D plural*
e.	*G sg masc*	j.	*I plural*

Ann--

C. THE NONSUFFIXED TYPE

This group contains eleven extremely common pronominal adjectives. They are:

1. the possessives мóй, твóй, свóй, нáш,
   вáш;
2. the demonstratives тóт, э́тот;
3. the determinatives вéсь, сáм;
4. the interrogative чéй;
5. the numeral одѝн.

(The ordinal numeral трéтий is often included in this
grouping, although strictly speaking it is suffixed.
That is, it is formed from the noun $tr\grave{e}t_z{+}\emptyset$ [f] by means
of the suffix $-j-$, giving $tr\acute{e}t_z/j{+}$.)
   There are several notations that must be made
about these pronominal adjectives because they deviate
in certain ways from the pattern outlined in the table
on p. 63. Since these deviations can be treated more
efficiently when the pronominal adjectives are grouped
according to the nature of the final consonant of the
stem, we will divide them in this way. Stems may end
in:

   a. a soft consonant

      moj+'   tvoj+'

      svoj+'   č/j+'

      v/ş+'

   b. a hard paired consonant

      t+'   ėt+

      sam+'   od/n+'

   c. a husher

      naš+   vaš+

The deviations mentioned above may now be summarized as follows:

(1)   End stress occurs only in Types a and b above.   (Remember that it never occurs at all in the suffixed pronominal adjectives.)   When end stress does occur, it results in absolute final stress in the di-syllabic endings of the singular (моего́, всему́), while in the plural the normal pattern of stress on the first syllable of an ending is observed (мои́ми, твои́ми, одни́ми).   Note that $sam+'$ has stress on the stem in the nominative plural: са́ми.

(2)   As noted in the table on p. 63, the ending $-oj$ (*fem sg* oblique case forms) is replaced by $-ej$ in all of the Type a pronominal adjectives (i.e., after any soft consonant):   мое́й, твое́й, свое́й, чье́й, все́й.

(3)   In the declension of $t+'$ and $v/\underset{\smile}{s}+'$ the vowel i in any ending is replaced by e: те́, все́, те́х, все́х, те́м, все́м, etc.

(4)   In the declension of pronominal adjectives of Type b (stem ending in a hard paired consonant), the fi-nal consonant of the stem unpredictably softens before any ending beginning with the vowel i (and, of course, its replacement e in the case of the pronominal adjec-tive $t+'$):   э́ти, одни́, са́ми, те́, э́тих, одни́х, сами́х, те́х, э́тим, одни́м, сами́м, etc.

(5)   The pronominal adjectives $t+'$ and $\acute{e}t+$ add $-ot$ instead of $-\emptyset$ in the *N sg masc*:   то́т, э́тот.

(6)   The fill vowel for $od/n+'$ is i instead of the expected o: оди́н.   In the other instances where a fill vowel occurs, the rules regarding the choice of vowel (Chapter 3, Section B) also apply.   Thus in both $\check{c}/j+'$ and $v/\underset{\smile}{s}+'$ the fill vowel is e: че́й, ве́сь.

QUESTIONS FOR THOUGHT AND DISCUSSION

1.   In what way(s) does the declension of pro-nominal adjectives differ from that of adjectives?

2.   Why is it necessary to make the statement about the ending $-oj$ becoming $-ej$ after a soft conso-nant only with regard to the pronominal adjectives and not for adjective declension as well?

3. What is ambiguous about forms such as прочий, сорочий, карий, курий, синий, олений?

4. Would any other form remove the ambiguity? Which form(s)? Explain.

5. Why does the vowel *i* occur so frequently as the fill vowel in pronominal adjective declension? In which pronominal adjectives does *e* occur as the fill vowel? Why does *o* not occur at all?

CHAPTER SIX

CONJUGATION

As was true of substantives in Russian, so it can be shown that for every *regular* Russian verb there is a single base form from which can be generated every possible form of that verb with its proper stress. In order to outline the manner in which this base form is derived, it will be necessary to make some preliminary statements about the composition of Russian words and specifically about verb forms.

The basic structure of Russian words contains the sequence prefix, root, suffix, ending. A stem is all of any given word minus the ending and will be indicated in our transcription, when necessary to divide it, by means of hyphens between the first three components (prefix, root, suffix) and a plus sign to indicate the separation of stem from ending. For example, the word проходи́ть would appear as *pro-xod̦-í+ț*.

A root in Russian generally follows the pattern CVC, with the first C representing any consonant or certain clusters of two or three consonants, the V any vowel unit, and the final C a single consonant or cluster of two consonants. The final consonant of a root is generally a hard paired consonant, a velar, or *j*; very rarely a husher or *c* may appear in final position, but this is usually the result of mutation. Occasionally, the first C or the V may be absent (VC or CC), but never in the same root. A small number of disyllabic roots (CVCVC) is also found.

Deviations from these general rules (for example, a missing final C) are usually explainable in terms of truncation, and the truncated consonant may be recovered from related forms. For instance, in the verbs затро́-нуть, засну́ть, and загну́ть we have in each case the prefix *za-* followed by a root that lacks a final consonant followed by the suffix *-nu*. The imperfective form of each verb (затра́гивать, засыпа́ть, загиба́ть) provides us information about that missing final consonant (*g*, *p*, and *b*, respectively).

   Since there is a relatively small number of prefixes, suffixes, and endings (i.e., in comparison with
the number of roots), all that is needed to begin an
analysis of the basic structure of verb forms is a listing of these prefixes, suffixes, and endings. Such a
listing follows.

VERBAL PREFIXES

v-	nad-	pŗed-
vz- (voz-)	ņiz-	pŗi-
vi-	o- (ob-)	pro-
do-	ot-	raz-
za-	ņeŗe- (pŗe-)	s-
iz-	po-	u-
na-	pod-	

   Prefixes that end in (or consist of) a consonant
will generally add *o* before nonsyllabic roots (i.e.,
roots that do not contain a vowel) or before certain
consonant clusters. Prefixes that end in *z* change this
consonant to *s* before voiceless consonants. In a perfective verb the stress will always be on the prefix
vi-.

VERBAL SUFFIXES

-a+	-o+	-ej+
-e+	-nu+	-ova+
-i+	-aj+	-vaj+

SUFFIXED PARTICLE

-şa *(after C)*   -ş *(after V)*

VERBAL ENDINGS

NONPAST TENSE

1st conj		*2nd conj*
-u	*1st sg*	-u
-oš	*2nd sg*	-iš
-ot	*3rd sg*	-it
-om	*1st pl*	-im
-oţe	*2nd pl*	-iţe
-ut	*3rd pl*	-at

PAST TENSE		INFINITIVE
masc	-l	-ţ
fem	-la	-ţi
neut	-lo	-č
pl	-ļi	

IMPERATIVE

-i

-∅

Before any ending which begins with *o*, *i*, or *a*, a paired consonant will automatically soften.

EXERCISE

Rewrite the following verbs in ST, indicating by means of hyphens and plus signs the division into prefixes, roots, suffixes, and endings:

Infinitive	*3rd pl, nonpast*[1]
1.	затихнуть	затихнут
2.	достроить	достроят
3.	отрезать	отрезают
4.	подстричь	подстригут
5.	заболеть	заболеют
6.	подковать	подкуют
7.	закрыть	закроют
8.	подпороть	подпорют
9.	прожрать	прожрут
10.	отвести	отведут
11.	выбросить	выбросят
12.	отдохнуть	отдохнут
13.	надышать	надышат
14.	замазать	замажут
15.	разуть	разуют
16.	возникнуть	возникнут
17.	упасти	упасут
18.	придумать	придумают
19.	украсть	украдут
20.	вздрогнуть	вздрогнут
21.	раздеть	разденут
22.	нажать	нажмут
23.	прервать	прервут
24.	отшлифовать	отшлифуют
25.	заслужить	заслужат
26.	продрожать	продрожат
27.	отвезти	отвезут
28.	завертеть	завертят
29.	отсечь	отсекут
30.	припомнить	припомнят
31.	отмахать	отмашут
32.	заскрипеть	заскрипят
33.	рассеять	рассеют
34.	зашить	зашьют
35.	укрепить	укрепят
36.	отрыть	отроют
37.	продуть	продуют
38.	отстоять	отстоят
39.	застонать	застонут
40.	переплыть	переплывут

---

[1]By nonpast is meant present or perfective future.

THE BASE FORM

The base form of any verb is determined in the following way. After comparing the stem of the infinitive with the stem of the nonpast tense (by means of an analysis similar to that done in the preceding exercise), we decide whether the verb is suffixed or not. If the verb does not contain a suffix, or if it contains either the suffix -*aj*+ or -*ej*+, then the base form is identical with the stem of the nonpast tense. If the verb is suffixed (with other than -*aj*+ or -*ej*+), then the base form is identical with the stem of the infinitive. (Remember that the stem of any word is all of that word minus the ending.)

Base forms will be divided by hyphens to indicate prefix, root, and suffix, and will end in a plus sign. Every base form will also contain a stress notation, detailed information about which is found on pp. 98-100.

The base form will also indicate the final truncated consonant of a root when that consonant is seen to appear in a related form. Thus the base forms of the three verbs discussed in the third paragraph of p. 72 would be *za-tróǵ-nu+*, *za-sṕ-nú+*, *za-gb́-nú+*.

Prefixes that end in *z* will be written with that letter in the base form, since the change of *z* to *s* is automatic before voiceless consonants.

EXERCISE

For each of the verbs on the preceding page decide whether the infinitive stem or the nonpast tense stem is basic.

A schematic representation of the classification of base forms by major and minor type is found below. Each of the various subtypes is represented by a brief letter designation of not more than three letters. Following this designation is a model verb that exemplifies the given subtype. A detailed analysis of each subtype is found on pp. 83-89 and 91-95; the aim of the schematic representation is to present in summary fashion the basic pattern of conjugational types.

VERB TYPES

The major division of verb types is based upon the presence or absence of a verbal suffix. Those verbs that do not have a suffix are called primary or nonsuffixed; those that possess a suffix are called secondary or suffixed.

PRIMARY VERBS

All primary verbs belong to the first conjugation. They may be subdivided into two groups according to the type of consonant that appears at the end of their base forms, a resonant consonant (v, j, r, m, n) or an obstruent consonant (d, t, z, s, b, g, k). Resonant stems are further subdivided into syllabic or nonsyllabic, depending on the presence or absence of a vowel in their root.

RESONANT

Syllabic		Nonsyllabic	
V	žĭv+	R	tŕ+
N	dén+	M/N	žḿ+
J	dúj+		

OBSTRUENT

D/T	vod+
Z/S	vož+
B	grob+
G/K	rok+

SECONDARY VERBS

Secondary verbs may be divided into two groups,
depending upon whether they belong to the first or second conjugation and further subdivided according to suffix.

FIRST CONJUGATION

A	ŗis-ǟ+	NU	kŗ̓ik-nu+
ns-A	žd-ǟ+	(NU)	sóx-(nu)+
OVA	tŗéb-ova+	AJ	čit-áj+
OV-A	kov-á+	EJ	krasŋ-éj+
O	kol-ǒ+	VAJ	da-váj+

SECOND CONJUGATION

I	proş-ǐ+	h-A	molč-á+
E	smotŗ-ě+	OJ-A	stoj-á+

It might be useful at this point to provide a
brief explanation of certain of the designations used
above. For reasons that will become clearer later, it
is necessary to distinguish between five different subtypes with the suffix -a+ and two with the suffix -nu+.
These distinctions may be summarized as follows:

A The suffix -a+ preceded by a root that ends
in a hard paired consonant, a velar or j.

ns-A The suffix -a+ preceded by a nonsyllabic
root.

OV-A The suffix -a+ preceded by a root that ends
in ov (as distinguished from the suffix -ova+, where the
ov is part of the suffix).

h-A The suffix -a+ preceded by a root that ends

in a husher.

   OJ-A   The suffix *-at* preceded by a root that ends
in *oj*.

   NU   The suffix *-nu+* which never truncates.

   (NU)   The suffix *-nu+* which truncates in certain
verb forms.

BASIC RULES OF COMBINATION

   All primary base forms end in a consonant, while
secondary base forms may end in either a consonant or a
vowel. All five vowels appear as the final element of a
suffix, but the only consonant that appears at the end
of a suffix is *j*. Since verbal endings may be either
consonantal or vocalic, and since base forms may end in
either a consonant or a vowel, when endings are added to
base forms any one of four possible combinations of vowel (V) and consonant (C) may occur: V+V, C+C, V+C, C+V.
When unlike elements combine (V+C, C+V), the result is
usually simple addition. The combination of like elements, on the other hand, usually results in some sort
of change and only rarely in simple addition. The most
common result of combining like elements is the truncation of the first one (V̸+V, C̸+C). This will be regarded
as normal and without need of special mention, whereas
deviations from this basic pattern will be noted for
each verb type.

EXERCISE

   In the following combinations of base forms and
endings, which involve truncation and which only simple
addition?

   1.   stoj-á̇+   *plus*   -iš   сто́йшь

   2.   klá̇d+   "   -u   кладу́

   3.   žd-ǎ̇+   "   -ḷi   жда́ли

   4.   čit-á̇j   "   -ot   чита́ет

5.	proṣ-ǐ+	*plus*	-it	прóсит
6.	kṛik-nu+	"	-la	крúкнула
7.	molč-á+	"	-at	молчáт
8.	žd-ǎ+	"	-u	ждý
9.	stoj-á+	"	-ḷi	стоя́ли
10.	da-váj+	"	-ṭ	давáть
11.	stán+	"	-ṭ	стáть
12.	tṛeb-ova+	"	-ḷi	трéбовали
13.	kṛik-nu+	"	-ut	крúкнут
14.	smotṛ-ě+	"	-im	смóтрим
15.	kol-ǒ+	"	-la	колóла
16.	klád+	"	-l	клáл
17.	stán+	"	-u	стáну
18.	čit-áj+	"	-la	читáла
19.	kol-ǒ	"	-oš	кóлешь
20.	krasṇ-éj+	"	-la	краснéла

In order to be able to generate the forms of the
infinitive, past, and nonpast tenses from any base form,
we will need to have, in addition to the basic rules of
combination noted on the preceding page, the following
items: (1) information about consonant mutation; (2)
comments about special alternations that affect only
certain verb types; and (3) some detailed information
about verb stress. These items will all be discussed
in the following sections.

CONSONANT MUTATION

In the environment V+V, when the second V is *o* or
u, the final consonant of the root of most verbs will
mutate according to the table listed below. Such mutation occurs in the first person singular of the nonpast
tense of *I* and *E* verbs and in *all* forms of the nonpast
tense of most secondary verbs of the first conjugation.
Note, however, that mutation does *not* occur in (1) *ns-A*
verbs; (2) *NU* or *(NU)* verbs; (3) the following *A* verbs:
žážd-a+, or-á+, sos-á+, ston-ã+. In *OVA* and *OV-A* verbs
mutation takes the form of a change of *-ov-* to *-uj-*.
Mutation also occurs in *I* and *E* verbs in both the past
passive verbal adjective (see p. 115, Item 2 under *FOR-
MATION*) and in the derived imperfective (see p. 121,
Item 1).

TABLE OF MUTATIONS

t	d	s	z	st	k	g	x	sk
č	ž	š	ž	šč	č	ž	š	šč

p	b	f	v	m	n	l	r
pḷ	bḷ	fḷ	vḷ	mḷ	ņ	ḷ	ŗ

1. If the consonant at the end of the root is not
one that mutates (e.g., *j*) or is the result of previous
mutation (e.g., one of the hushers), then obviously no
mutation will occur.
2. In a few verbs *t* and *d* mutate to *šč* and *žd*.
Such instances must be noted in the base form. In the
first person singular, nonpast tense, only *ž* appears.

3. Either the hard or soft variant of any paired consonant will result in the mutations listed above. Thus, s or $ş$ becomes $š$, z or $ʐ$ becomes $ž$, etc.

4. The change of g/k to $ž/č$ before o (occurring in velar obstruent primary stems and in the ns-A verb lg-$ả$+) is not V+V mutation, but a special alternation that affects only the velars.

STRESS

Stress in the nonpast tense forms is either fixed or shifting. If the former, it can be fixed either on the stem or on the endings. If shifting, there is only one possibility: stress on the ending in the first person singular with a shift to the next preceding syllable in all other forms of the nonpast tense.

EXERCISE

Which of the following verbs have fixed stress, and which have shifting stress? Which of the former have end stress, and which have stem stress?

1. несу́, несёшь
2. ста́ну, ста́нешь
3. по́мню, по́мнишь
4. терплю́, те́рпишь
5. говорю́, говори́шь
6. тяну́, тя́нешь
7. ре́жу, ре́жешь
8. умру́, умрёшь
9. покажу́, пока́жешь
10. откро́ю, откро́ешь

Stress in the past tense may likewise be either fixed or shifting. If fixed, the stress is constant on the stem or on the endings. If shifting, there is only one pattern possible: stress on the ending in the feminine form and on a syllable of the stem in the other three forms.

EXERCISE

Which of the following verbs have fixed stress, and which have shifting stress? Which of the former have end stress, and which have stem stress?

1.   стри́г, стри́гла, стри́гли
2.   ду́мал, ду́мала, ду́мали
3.   плы́л, плыла́, плы́ли
4.   у́мер, умерла́, у́мерли
5.   нёс, несла́, несли́
6.   тяну́л, тяну́ла, тяну́ли
7.   откры́л, откры́ла, откры́ли
8.   жда́л, ждала́, жда́ли
9.   тёк, текла́, текли́
10. по́нял, поняла́, по́няли

VERB TYPE ANALYSIS

PRIMARY VERBS

   1.   RESONANT

      a.   SYLLABIC STEMS

V type — ži̯v+, pli̯v+, sli̯v+.

N type — ḑen+, stan+, stin+, -stran+.[1]

J type — du̯j+, gṛej+, -u̯j+, -či̯j+, gṇi̯j+.

In all of these verb types there are no unpredictable changes in the formation of the infinitive or the past and nonpast tenses. The expected truncation of the final consonant (∅+C) is seen in the infinitive and past tense, while the vocalic endings of the nonpast tense are simply added to the base form:

---

[1]The presence of a hyphen preceding the base form signifies that the verb being cited never occurs without a prefix.

žĭv+ *plus* -ṭ, -1, -u, -oš = жи́ть, жи́л,
                                     живу́, живёшь

q̧en+   "   -ṭ, -1, -u, -oš = де́ть, де́л,
                                     де́ну, де́нешь

dúj+   "   -ṭ, -1, -u, -oš = ду́ть, ду́л,
                                     ду́ю, ду́ешь

STRESS COMMENTS

Stress in the nonpast tense of syllabic resonant primary stems is always fixed either on the stem (*N* and *J* types) or on the endings. (Exception: $gn\overset{x}{i}j$+ with end stress in the nonpast tense.) Stress in the past tense may be either fixed on the stem or shifting.

Since nonpast tense stress is never shifting, and since the place of stress is determined by the final element of the base form (*n* or *j* imply stem stress, *v* end stress), we need signify only the past tense stress pattern. The symbol (') will be used to indicate that stress in the past tense is fixed on the syllable over which that symbol appears, while the symbol (^{x}) will be used to indicate shifting stress in the past tense. This shift will always oppose the ending in the feminine form to either the root vowel or the vowel of the prefix, and the placing of our symbol will indicate this (u-$pl\overset{x}{i}v$+; $pr\overset{x}{o}$-$\check{z}iv$+). Regardless of which type of stress is indicated, the place of stress in the infinitive form of *all* resonant primary stems is the root vowel.

There are two special subtypes of *J* verbs, each with an unpredictable alternation. They are:

OJ — mój+, vój+, krój+, nój+, rój+.

In these five verbs the *o* of the root becomes *i* when any consonantal ending is added. This is in addition to the expected truncation of the final consonant.

IJ — ҏ$\overset{x}{i}$j+, ḅij+, v̧$\overset{x}{i}$j+, ḷ$\overset{x}{i}$j+, šij+.

In these five verbs the *i* of the base form drops when any vocalic ending is added. Before consonantal endings there is only the expected truncation of the final consonant:

$$\text{mój+ } plus \quad -t̡, \ -1, \ -u, \ -oš \ = \ \text{МЫ́ТЬ, МЫ́Л,}$$
$$\text{МО́Ю, МО́ЕШЬ}$$

$$\text{p̡íj+ } \quad " \quad -t̡, \ -1, \ -u, \ -oš \ = \ \text{ПИ́ТЬ, ПИ́Л,}$$
$$\text{ПЬЮ́, ПЬЁШЬ}$$

STRESS COMMENTS

No special problems arise as long as it is kept in mind that when the vowel i of the IJ subtype drops out, the root becomes nonsyllabic, and stress must of necessity fall on the endings in the nonpast tense.

b. NONSYLLABIC STEMS

R type — tŕ+, mŕ+, pŕ+, -stŕ+.

In verbs of this type there are unpredictable alternations before consonantal endings (C+C). Instead of truncation of the final consonant, we find that the final r becomes $eṛé$ before the infinitive ending, while before any other consonantal ending r becomes or. In addition, when the past tense endings are added, the masculine $-l$ truncates (C+∅), but the other past tense endings are simply added without any truncation.[1]

$$\text{tŕ+ } plus \quad -t̡, \ -1, \ -la, \ -u, \ -oš \ = \ \text{ТЕРЕ́ТЬ,}$$
$$\text{ТЁР, ТЁРЛА,}$$
$$\text{ТРУ́, ТРЁШЬ}$$

M/N type — žḿ+, žń+, mń+, -pń+, -čń+.

The only deviation that occurs among verbs of this type is the unpredictable change of final m/n to a when any consonantal ending is added.

---

[1]The truncation of the past masculine ending $-l$, and the simple addition of the other consonantal endings without truncation, occurs elsewhere and will be referred to hereafter as the *special C+C deviation*.

žm̍+ *plus* -t̡, -l, -u, -oš =   жа́ть, жа́л,
                                   жму́, жмёшь

mn̍+   "   -t̡, -l, -u, -oš   мя́ть, мя́л,
                                   мну́, мнёшь

There is in addition a special subtype of the *M/N*
type (the *ŊM* subtype) which requires several explana-
tory comments. When a consonantal prefix (i.e., one
ending in or consisting of a consonant) is added to a
verb of this subtype, the vowel *i* is inserted in the
root before any vocalic ending, and the stress pattern
of the nonpast tense is shifting. (Stress shift in the
nonpast tense of a primary verb is a major deviation.)
On the other hand, when a vocalic prefix (one that ends
in or consists of a vowel) is added, the *ŋ̡* of the root
becomes *j* before any vocalic ending. As expected, before any consonantal ending the final *m* becomes ͵*a*.

s-ŋ̂m̍+ *plus* -t̡, -l, -u, -oš =   снять, сня́л,
                                    сниму́, сни́мешь

pŏ̆-ŋm+   "   -t̡, -l, -u, -oš =   поня́ть, по́-
                                нял, пойму́, поймёшь

STRESS COMMENTS

Since stress in the nonpast tense of nonsyllabic
stems is of necessity fixed on the endings, there is no
question about the place of stress in those forms, and
our symbol here, as in the syllabic stems, refers to the
past tense pattern. Thus the stress comments on p. 84
will also apply here. It should be added that the reference to root vowel in those comments implies, for nonsyllabic resonant stems, that vowel which develops when
consonantal endings are added (that is, ͵*a* in the *M/N*
type verbs, and the second *e* of *e̡re̡* in *R* type verbs).
For example, note the place of stress in the infinitive
form of the following verbs:

nă̆-čn+   нача́ть
pŏ̆-ŋm+   поня́ть
ză̆-pr+   запере́ть
na-žm̍+   нажа́ть

2. OBSTRUENT

a. NONVELAR STEMS

D/T type — v̧od+, klad+, m̧ot+, cv̧ot+ *(plus about ten more)*.

The only unpredictable alternation found in this type is the change of d/t to s before the infinitive ending.

v̧od+ *plus* -ţi, -1, -u, -oš = вести́, вёл, веду́, ведёшь

klad+   "   -ţ, -1, -u, -oš = кла́сть, кла́л, кладу́, кладёшь

Z/S type — v̧oż+, griz+, ņoś+ *(plus four others)*.

The only unpredictable alternation found in this type is the special C+C deviation (see footnote, p. 85).

v̧oż+ *plus* -ţi, -1, -la, -u = везти́, вёз, везла́, везу́

griz+   "   -ţ, -1, -la, -u = гры́зть, гры́з, гры́зла, грызу́

ņoś+   "   -ţi, -1, -la, -u = нести́, нёс, несла́, несу́

B type — gŗob+, skŗob+

Verbs of this type share deviations with the two groups above in that before the infinitive ending the final b changes to s (as in the D/T type), while before other consonantal endings we find the special C+C deviation (as in the Z/S type).

gŗob+   *plus*   -ţi, -1, -la, -u = грести́, грёб, гребла́, гребу́

b. VELAR STEMS

G/K type — p̦ok̓+, țok̓+, str̦ig+ *(plus about ten others).*

Verbs of this type exhibit the special C+C deviation in the past tense; however, the combination of velar with infinitive ending results in -č (spelled чь), before which a root vowel ₑo changes to ₑe.[1] Another unpredictable alternation is the mutation of *g/k* to *ž/č* before any ending that begins with *o*.[2]

p̦ok̓+ *plus* -ț, -1, -1a, -u, -oš = пе́чь, пёк,
                     пекла́, пеку́, печёшь

str̦ig+ "   -ț, -1, -1a, -u, -oš = стри́чь,
             стри́г, стри́гла, стригу́, стрижёшь

c. NONSYLLABIC STEMS

There are two regular nonsyllabic obstruent stems (žg+, -čt+) which require comment only with regard to the insertion of a fill vowel in certain forms. Whenever a zero ending, or an ending that does not contain a vowel, is added to the base form of these verbs, a fill vowel appears. This vowel is regularly *o* (spelled ё) which expectedly changes to *e* in the infinitive. For example:

žg+   *plus* -ț, -1, -1a, -u = же́чь, жёг,
                      жгла́, жгу́

pro-čt+ "   -ț, -1, -1a, -u = проче́сть,
             прочёл, прочла́, прочту́

----

[1]For a discussion of the alternation of *o* and *e* in conjugation, see Item 1 on p. 125.

[2]The same mutation occurs in the *ns-A* verb *lg-ã+*, i.e., лгу́, лжёшь, лжёт, лжём, лжёте, лгу́т. See Item 4, p. 82.

STRESS COMMENTS

Stress in the nonpast tense of all regular obstruent primary stems is always fixed on the endings, while
past tense stress may be fixed either on the stem or on
the endings. (Exceptions: In the nonpast tense the
verb *mog̀+* has shifting stress, and the verb *l̦éz+* has
stem stress.) Since shifting stress does not occur in
any regular obstruent primary stem, we need only the one
symbol ('). Placing this symbol over the final consonant in the base form signals end stress in the past
tense and implies, at the same time, the stressed infinitive ending −ТИ́ for nonvelar stems. (Velar stems have
−ЧЬ regardless of the stress.) Placing the symbol over
the penultimate element in the base form signals fixed
stress on that syllable in the past tense and infinitive
and implies as well the infinitive ending −ТЬ for nonvelar stems. Stress in the infinitive form of velar
stems is always on the syllable preceding the ending
−ЧЬ.

No stress symbol is actually needed for nonsyllabic obstruent stems, since in the nonpast and past tenses
of these verbs the stress can only be on the endings,
while stress in their infinitives is always on the root
vowel (i.e., the fill vowel).

EXERCISE

Be prepared to generate the infinitive and past
and nonpast tenses of the following verbs:

1.	za-gríz+	8.	pro-žg+
2.	ob-új+	9.	dǒ-živ+
3.	raz-mń+	10.	za-pļót+
4.	ǒt-pr+	11.	s-čt+
5.	pro-gṛob+	12.	pod-rój+
6.	raz-krój+	13.	po-pád+
7.	za-ḫíj+	14.	ǔ-mr+

15.   pod-žm̍+   23.   u-vl̩ok̍+

16.   za-pr̩ag̍+   24.   pro-str̍+

17.   pr̩i-vọž̍+   25.   na-dúj+

18.   o-ḓen̍+   26.   v-vọd̍+

19.   do-str̩ig̍+   27.   pŏ̌d-ŋm̍+

20.   u-plǐv+   28.   s-pas̍+

21.   ṟěṟe-ŋm+   29.   pr̩i-ṿǐj+

22.   prǒ̌-l̩ij+   30.   pro-ṱok̍+

EXERCISE

The following questions refer to the verbs in the preceding exercise:

1.   To what basic type and subtype do each of these verbs belong?

2.   How do you account for the different spellings (in Cyrillic) of the prefix *raz-* in Nos. 3 and 6?

3.   Explain the insertion of *o* in spelling the non-past tense forms of Nos. 3, 4, and 15? Why is *o* not inserted in spelling the infinitive or past tense of those verbs?

4.   Why is no stress mark used in Nos. 8 and 11?

5.   All of the primary stems with the shifting symbol ($^{\times}$) belong to which basic type?

6.   Why is this symbol not used with obstruent stems?

7.   What are the three possible infinitive endings for obstruent stems?

8.   How do you know which ending to choose?

9.   Could you ignore the stress symbol in generating any of the forms for the preceding exercise?
Which forms? Explain.

10.   What special notations (i.e., in addition to
the basic rules of combination found on p. 79) did you
have to apply to generate the correct forms of Nos.

      a.   1, 17, and 28;
      b.   3 and 15;
      c.   4, 14, and 24;
      d.   10, 13, and 26;
      e.   16, 19, 23, and 30;
      f.   21 and 27;
      g.   6 and 12;
      h.   7, 22, and 29;
      i.   8 and 11?

SECONDARY VERBS

STRESS COMMENTS

Although we will make use of the same symbols that
were used to indicate stress in primary verbs, their implications for secondary verbs will be somewhat different. In primary stems the stress mark was placed either
over the prefix or over the root in the base form; in
secondary stems it will be placed either over the root
or over the suffix. The symbol (') can be placed in either of these two positions, while the symbol (×) can
appear only over the suffix.
When the symbol (') is placed over the root it
signifies fixed stress on that syllable in all forms of
the verb. When it is placed over the suffix it signifies fixed stress on the post-root syllable in all forms
of the verb, i.e., on the suffix in the past tense and
infinitive (in other words, before consonantal endings),
but on the endings in the nonpast tense of those verbs
in which the suffix, or a portion of it, truncates before vocalic endings (V+V). If the suffix remains in-
tact before vocalic endings (i.e., in verbs with the
suffix -aj+ or -ej+), then the fixed symbol signifies
fixed stress on the suffix (therefore on the stem)
in all forms of the verb. The symbol (×), when placed

over the suffix in the base form, indicates stress on
that syllable in the past tense and infinitive, but a
shifting pattern in the nonpast tense. (For details of
this pattern, see p. 82.)

EXCEPTIONS

1. In verbs of the *OVA* type, although stress may
fall on the second syllable of the suffix, and although
this vowel truncates before the vocalic endings of the
nonpast tense, nevertheless the nonpast tense stress
does not fall on the endings. It falls instead on the
syllable that replaces *-ov-*, that is, on the *u* of *-uj-*.

2. In *ns-A* verbs, which all have end stress in
the nonpast tense, the symbol (ˣ) refers to past tense
stress. These verbs are the only regular secondary
stems which admit shifting stress in the past tense.
However, since *ns-A* verbs are readily identified, and
since they must have end stress in their nonpast tense,
the use of the symbol (ˣ) to indicate shifting past
tense stress in a secondary verb does not present any
possibility of ambiguity.

SECONDARY VERBS

1. FIRST CONJUGATION

A type — ɲis-ǎ+ *(around seventy-five stems)*

V+V mutation occurs where possible in all but four
stems (see p. 81). Stress may be fixed (on stem or
endings) or shifting, but end stress and V+V mutation
never co-occur.

ns-A type — žd-ǎ+ *(fifteen stems)*

No V+V mutation in regular verbs of this type.
Stress is always fixed on the endings in the nonpast
tense, and all but two have shifting stress in the past
tense. In three verbs (*br-ǎ+*, *dr-ǎ+*, *zv-ǎ+*) an *o* is inserted in the root when vocalic endings are added. This
o causes the preceding consonant to soften in the first

two of these verbs, but not in the third (i.e., беру́, берёшь; деру́, дерёшь; but зову́, зовёшь).

OVA type — tr̦e̍b-ova+ *(thousands)*

V+V mutation occurs, taking the form of a change of *-ov-* to *-uj-*. Stress is always fixed either on a syllable of the root or on the second syllable of the suffix (e.g., *d̦ikt-ová+*). In this latter instance, nonpast tense stress is never on the endings (i.e., it falls on the *-uj-*).

OV-A type — kov-a̍+ *(seven stems)*

V+V mutation occurs, taking the form of a change of *-ov-* to *-uj-*. Stress symbol is always on the suffix, with nonpast tense stress fixed on the endings.

O type — kol-o̽+, pol-o̽+, por-o̽+, mol-o̽+, bor-o̽+șa

V+V mutation occurs in all verbs of this type. Nonpast tense stress is always shifting.

NU type — kr̦i̍k-nu+ *(hundreds)*

No V+V mutation. Stress may be fixed (stem or endings) or shifting. There may or may not be a consonant preceding the suffix *-nu+*, and the absence of a consonant implies an earlier truncation (see p. 72).

(NU) type — so̍x-(nu)+ *(around sixty stems)*

No V+V mutation. The suffix *-nu+* truncates before any consonantal ending except either the infinitive ending *-ț* or the past passive verbal adjective desinence *-t*. The special C+C deviation also occurs in the past tense. Stress is always fixed on the root vowel, and there will always be a consonant preceding the suffix *-nu+*. (The only exception to this is the stem *-v̦ád̸-(nu)+*, where even though the final root consonant has truncated, the *-nu+* still drops. For example, from the

verb *za-ųáḍ-(nu)+* we have the past tense forms завя́л,
завя́ла, завя́ло, завя́ли.)

   AJ type — čit-áj+ *(thousands)*

   Stress is always fixed either on the root or on
the suffix.

   EJ type — krasņ-éj+ *(hundreds)*

   Stress is almost always fixed on the suffix.   (The
major exceptions comprise a sizable group of verbs with
the compound prefix *o-ḅez-*.   These verbs always have
stress on the root vowel, e.g., обезлю́деть, обез-
ле́сеть.)

   VAJ type — da-váj+, -zna-váj+, -sta-váj+

   In the nonpast tense the *-va-* of the suffix drops,
and stress is fixed on the endings.

   2.   SECOND CONJUGATION

   I type — proş-í̆+ *(thousands)*

   V+V mutation.   Stress may be fixed (stem or endings) or shifting.

   E type — smotŗ-ĕ̆+ *(around fifty stems)*

   V+V mutation.   Stress may be fixed (stem or endings) or shifting.

   h-A type — molč-á+ *(around thirty stems)*

   Stress may be fixed (stem or endings) or shifting.

   OJ-A type — stoj-á+, boj-á+şa
   Stress always fixed on endings in nonpast tense.

EXAMPLES OF SECONDARY STEMS

Base form plus the endings -ţ, -l, -la, -u, -oš:

p̦is-ä̇+	писа́ть, писа́л, писа́ла, пишу́, пи́шешь
žd-ä̇+	жда́ть, жда́л, ждала́, жду́, ждёшь
tr̦eb-ova+	тре́бовать, тре́бовал, тре́бовала, тре́бую, тре́буешь
kov-ȧ+	кова́ть, кова́л, кова́ла, кую́, куёшь
kol-ŏ+	коло́ть, коло́л, коло́ла, колю́, ко́лешь
kr̦ik-nu+	кри́кнуть, кри́кнул, кри́кнула, кри́кну, кри́кнешь
sox-(nu)+	со́хнуть, со́х, со́хла, со́хну, со́хнешь
čit-aj+	чита́ть, чита́л, чита́ла, чита́ю, чита́ешь
krasņ-ej+	красне́ть, красне́л, красне́ла, красне́ю, красне́ешь
da-vaj+	дава́ть, дава́л, дава́ла, даю́, даёшь
proș-ï+	проси́ть, проси́л, проси́ла, прошу́, про́сишь
smotr̦-ě+	смотре́ть, смотре́л, смотре́ла, смотрю́, смо́тришь
molč-ȧ+	молча́ть, молча́л, молча́ла, молчу́, молчи́шь
stoj-ȧ+	стоя́ть, стоя́л, стоя́ла, стою́, стои́шь
krap-a+	кра́пать, кра́пал, кра́пала, кра́плю, кра́плешь
žr-ä̇+	жра́ть, жра́л, жрала́, жру́, жрёшь
atak-ovȧ+	атакова́ть, атакова́л, атакова́ла, атаку́ю, атаку́ешь
kļov-ȧ+	клева́ть, клева́л, клева́ла, клюю́, клюёшь
gļäd-nu+	гля́нуть, гля́нул, гля́нула, гля́ну, гля́нешь
ḑerž-ä̇+	держа́ть, держа́л, держа́ла, держу́, де́ржишь
stroj-i+	стро́ить, стро́ил, стро́ила, стро́ю, стро́ишь

EXERCISES

1.   Identify by basic type each of the verbs in
the exercise on p. 75. In which of those verbs does V+V
mutation occur?

2.   Be prepared to generate the infinitive and
past and nonpast tenses of the following verbs:

1.   pod-d̦el-aj+   16.   pro-n̦ik-(nu)+

2.   u-kr̨ep̨-i̦+   17.   pod-čist̨-i+

3.   o-sm̨ej-a̦+   18.   do-v̨ert̨-ě+

4.   s-kid̨-nu+   19.   u-gad-a̦j+

5.   pod-rv-ǎ+   20.   vi̦-žd-a+

6.   na-v̨az-ǎ+   21.   na-korm̨-ǐ+

7.   za-vlad̨-ėj+   22.   za-bol̨-ė+

8.   p̨er̨e-stoj-a̦+   23.   v-sov-a̦+

9.   pro-s̨id̨-ė+   24.   raz-max-ǎ+

10.   raz-máz-a+   25.   za-t̨ix-(nu)+

11.   za-d̨erž-ǎ+   26.   pro-t̨ag̦-nǔ+

12.   ot-táj-a+   27.   raz-sli̦š-a+

13.   do-pol-ǒ+   28.   u-sta-va̦j+

14.   za-mk-nú+   29.   na-diš-ǎ+

15.   iz-bal-ova̦+   30.   pr̨i-zna-va̦j+

3.   The following questions refer to the verbs
above:

1.   To which basic type and subtype does each verb
belong?

2.   In which verbs does V+V mutation occur in all
forms of the nonpast tense?   In which does it occur in
only the first person singular of the nonpast tense?

3.   Explain the insertion of *o* in all forms of
No. 5.

4.   Explain the different place of stress in the
nonpast tense forms of Nos. 15 and 23.

SUMMARY

As can be seen from the table of verb endings on
p. 74 , all nonpast tense endings are vocalic, while
past tense and infinitive endings are consonantal.   Of
the four vowels that may appear as the first element of
a vocalic ending (*a*, *i*, *o*, *u*), before the first three a
paired consonant will always be soft.   Only before *u* is
it possible for a paired consonant to be hard, and when
a soft paired consonant appears before *u*, this is an indication of V+V mutation.

The choice of infinitive ending depends on the
verb type.   All secondary verbs and all resonant primary
verbs have the ending -t_{i}, which is always preceded by a
vowel.   Nonvelar obstruent primary verbs have -$t_{i}i$ or -t_{i}
depending on the stress pattern of the past tense (end
stress implies the former, stem stress the latter).
Note that -t_{i} here will always be preceded by a consonant.   Velar obstruent primary verbs have the ending -*č*
in the infinitive.

The combination of unlike elements (V+C, C+V) is
said to be a stable environment where no problems are
expected to arise when base forms and endings are
joined.   Thus the addition of infinitive and past tense
endings to secondary verbs (V+C) is completely unproblematical, except for the truncation of the suffix -*nut*
in *(NU)* verbs and the appearance of shifting stress in
the past tense of *ns-A* verbs.   The addition of nonpast
tense endings to primary verbs (C+V) is likewise without
major deviations from the basic rules, except for the
mutation of velars before *o*, the loss of *i* in the *IJ*
subtype, and shifting stress in *NM* verbs with a consonantal prefix.   But when past tense and infinitive endings are added to primary verbs (C+C), we find stress

shift (past tense of certain resonant primary stems) and many deviations from the truncation rules (past tense and infinitive of obstruents, nonsyllabic resonants, and verbs of the *OJ* subtype). Similarly, when nonpast tense endings are added to secondary verbs (V+V), stress shift and V+V mutation are seen to occur in certain types of verbs.

STRESS SUMMARY

1. RESONANT STEMS. Verbs of the *N* and *J* types have stem stress in the nonpast tense;[1] all other types have end stress.[2] Past tense stress may be either fixed on the root vowel or shifting. If the latter, stress is often attracted to the prefix in the nonfeminine forms of the past tense. Stress in the infinitive is always on the root vowel, regardless of the past tense stress pattern.

2. OBSTRUENT STEMS. End stress is general in the nonpast tense.[3] About eighty percent of these verbs have end stress in the past tense as well.[4] Stress on the infinitive ending (-ТЍ) occurs only among syllabic nonvelar stems with end stress in the past tense. All other obstruent stems have stress on the root vowel in the infinitive form.

3. SECONDARY STEMS. Past tense is always fixed on the stem.[5] Shifting stress in the nonpast tense occurs only among *A*, *O*, *NU*, *I*, *E*, and *h-A* verbs. The remaining types thus never have shifting stress anywhere.

Certain secondary verbs have only end stress in the nonpast tense (*ns-A*, *OV-A*, *VAJ*, *OJ-A*); others have only stem stress (*AJ*, *EJ*, *(NU)*, *OVA*). Only *A*, *NU*, *I*, *E*,

---

[1]Except for *gņi̽j+* with end stress.

[2]Except that *ŅM* verbs with a consonantal prefix have shifting stress.

[3]Except *ļéz+* with stem stress and *moǵ+* with shifting stress.

[4]The verb *pŗa̽d+* is the only obstruent stem with shifting past tense stress. However, variants with stem stress (base form *pŗád+*) are also sanctioned.

[5]Except for *ns-A* verbs with shifting stress.

and *h-A* verbs admit all three possibilities of nonpast
tense stress (stem, end, or shifting); *O* verbs have only
shifting stress. Verbs of the *A* type with V+V mutation
in their nonpast tense never have end stress, only stem
or shifting stress.

Stress in the infinitive form of all secondary
verbs is always on the syllable over which the stress
mark is placed in the base form.

4. PLACING THE STRESS MARK IN THE BASE FORM.
Let us regard as normal the situation wherein all primary verbs have fixed stress in their nonpast tense forms,
and all secondary verbs have fixed stress in their past
tense forms. Let us also regard as normal the fact that
shifting stress may occur only in the past tense of primary verbs and in the nonpast tense of secondary verbs.
If we also keep in mind the fact that all primary verbs
except those in *N* or *J* have fixed end stress, then we
may operate with only two symbols for stress notation:
(') for fixed stress and (×) for shifting stress. (The
few exceptions to all of the above generalizations have
been noted earlier.)

The fixed stress mark (') on a secondary base form
informs us that the syllable over which it appears is
always stressed in the past, nonpast, and infinitive
forms. The mark (×) on a secondary base form means that
that syllable is stressed in the past tense and infinitive, but that there is shifting stress in the nonpast
tense.[1]

In placing the stress mark on primary verbs we
must keep in mind the fact that the stress symbol says
nothing about the stress of the nonpast tense, since
that information is provided by the base form itself.
(That is, end stress in all primary verbs except those
in *N* or *J*.) Thus the stress mark on a primary base form
refers to past tense and infinitive, *not* to the nonpast
tense.

If the verb is a resonant, then the (') indicates
that stress is fixed on that syllable in the infinitive
and past tense. The symbol (×), whether placed over the
root or the prefix, signifies stress on that syllable in

---

[1]Exceptions: (1) in *OVA* verbs, *-ová+* always implies stress on *-új-*, not on the endings in the nonpast;
(2) in *ns-A* verbs the (×) refers to past tense stress.

the nonfeminine forms of the past tense and end stress
in the feminine form. The stress in the infinitive will
always be on the root vowel, regardless of where the
symbol is placed in the base form.

If the verb is an obstruent, then only the mark
(') is needed, and its position indicates both the place
of stress in the past tense (stem or endings), as well
as the choice of ending in the infinitive of nonvelar
stems (-ТИ or ТЬ).

EXERCISE MATERIAL

The hypothetical base forms listed below are to be
used in several subsequent exercises requiring you to
generate certain forms of these verbs. Be sure to write
the requested forms in Cyrillic with the correct stress
on each one. Each base form represents an imperfective
verb; the prefix following it is to be used to form the
perfective aspect.

1. pră̆v+   /u-   14. zad-aj+   /vi-

2. gor-ŏ̆+   /pod-   15. br̍+   /s-

3. skop-ě̆+   /na-   16. trat+   /na-

4. s̨i̊j+   /nad-   17. glož-ǎ̆+   /raz-

5. l̨ok̍+   /ot-   18. trun+   /po-

6. muz̨-ėj+   /v-   19. dad+   /za-

7. tak-ova̍+   /per̨e-   20. st̨ėj+   /u-

8. gd-ǎ̆+   /ob-   21. kn̨ig-a+   /na-

9. lȯj+   /do-   22. p̨ik-(nu)+   /pro-

10. blat̨-i̊+   /pro-   23. kamn̨-e+   /pod-

11. pok-ǎ̆+   /u-   24. l̨ud̨-i+   /u-

12. šn̍+   /pod-   25. bov-a̍+   /pro-

13. stog-nu̍+   /pr̨i-

EXERCISE

For each of the verbs on the preceding page, give
the following forms: (1) infinitive; (2) 1st sg nonpast; (3) 3rd sg nonpast; (4) 3rd pl nonpast; (5) past
masculine; (6) past feminine; (7) past plural. (Give
only imperfective forms for this exercise.)

IMPERATIVE

ENDING

The imperative is formed by adding the ending $-i$
to the base form. This ending is replaced by $-\emptyset$ in all
verbs which have fixed stem stress in the nonpast tense
and a *nonpast* stem ending in a single consonant.[1] The
following additional facts must be noted:

(1)   Not only before $-i$, but also before $-\emptyset$, a
paired consonant will automatically be soft.

ņos̍+	неси́	žĭv+	живи́
sta̍n+	стань	vȩr̦-i+	верь

(2)   Verbs which have a change in the stem in *all*
forms of the nonpast tense (V+V mutation, insertion of a
vowel, etc.) will have this change in the imperative
form as well.

p̦is-ă̆+	пиши́	tȓeb-ova+	тре́буй
ŏt-ņm+	отними́	zv-ă̆+	зови́

---

[1]Note that perfective verbs with the prefix vi-
must be analyzed without that prefix in order to deter-
mine their proper stress pattern, since this prefix always attracts the stress when forming a perfective verb.
Thus $vi̱-stav̦-i+$ is truly stem stressed ($sta̍v̦-i+$), but
$vi̱-govor̦-i+$ is not ($govor̦-i̍+$), and their corresponding
imperative forms reflect this difference: вы́ставь,
but вы́говори.

(3) Verbs of the *IJ* subtype expectedly insert a fill vowel in their nonsyllabic nonpast tense stem.

p̞ĭ̌j+ (nonpast stem p̞j-)   пе́й

EXCEPTIONS

1. The expected -*i* is replaced by -∅ in

    a. *OV-A* and *OJ-A* verbs, and the stem -sm̩ej-á+.

    b. *VAJ* verbs, which add the -∅ to the base form with no loss of -*va*- (e.g., дава́й). Thus *VAJ* verbs do not follow Rule 2, above.

2. The verb *sı́p-a+* has сы́пь instead of the expected *сы́пли.

STRESS

Verbs with stress fixed on the stem in the nonpast tense will have stress on the same syllable in their imperative forms, regardless of whether the imperative ending is -*i* or -∅. In all other instances (i.e., fixed end stress or shifting stress) the imperative ending will be stressed. Note that stress which (morphophonemically) falls on a zero ending (*stoj*-∅ from *stoj*-á+, *kuj*+∅ from *kov*-á+) will always have to be pronounced on the preceding syllable (сто́й, ку́й, etc.).

EXAMPLES

Stressed -*i*

plı̌v+	плыви́	v̞oz+	вези́
žm̩+	жми́	p̞ok+	пеки́
tr̩+	три́	žg+	жги́
p̞is-ã+	пиши́	pros̞-ı̌+	проси́
žd-ã+	жди́	gl̩ad̞-e+	гляди́

kol-ŏ̌+	коли́	molč-a̍+	молчи́
max-ǎ+	маши́	ţaǿ-nǔ+	тяни́

Unstressed -i

kri̩k-nu+	кри́кни	ko̍nč-i+	ко́нчи
po̍mņ-i+	по́мни	so̍x-(nu)+	со́хни

Stressed -∅

kov-a̍+	ку́й	stoj-a̍+	сто́й
sṃej-a̍+şa	сме́йся	boj-a̍+şa	бо́йся

Unstressed -∅

sta̍n+	ста́нь	čit-a̍j+	чита́й
mo̍j+	мо́й	krasņ-e̍j+	красне́й

EXERCISES

1. Generate an imperative form for each of the
verbs in the exercises on pp. 89-90.

2. Generate an imperative for each of the verbs
listed on p. 96.

(In doing the two exercises above, be sure to
write each form in Cyrillic with its proper stress.)

3. Provide a base form (in ST with the proper
stress symbol) for each of the verbs listed on the following two pages. (The forms provided are: infinitive;
1st and 2nd singular, nonpast; and past tense masculine,
feminine, and plural.)

1. вскры́ть, вскро́ю, вскро́ешь, вскры́л,
   вскры́ла, вскры́ли.
2. вспоро́ть, вспорю́, вспо́решь, вспоро́л,
   вспоро́ла, вспоро́ли
3. доказа́ть, докажу́, дока́жешь, доказа́л,
   доказа́ла, доказа́ли.
4. заду́ть, заду́ю, заду́ешь, заду́л, заду́ла,
   заду́ли.
5. заже́чь, зажгу́, зажжёшь, зажёг, зажгла́,
   зажгли́.
6. заноси́ть, заношу́, зано́сишь, заноси́л,
   заноси́ла, заноси́ли.
7. запере́ть, запру́, запрёшь, за́пер, заперла́,
   за́перли
8. запря́тать, запря́чу, запря́чешь, запря́тал,
   запря́тала, запря́тали
9. затяну́ть, затяну́, затя́нешь, затяну́л,
   затяну́ла, затяну́ли
10. наня́ть, найму́, наймёшь, на́нял, наняла́,
    на́няли.
11. насе́ять, насе́ю, насе́ешь, насе́ял,
    насе́яла, насе́яли
12. обду́мать, обду́маю, обду́маешь, обду́мал,
    обду́мала, обду́мали
13. обня́ть, обниму́, обни́мешь, о́бнял, обняла́,
    о́бняли.
14. обыска́ть, обыщу́, обы́щешь, обыска́л,
    обыска́ла, обыска́ли
15. овладе́ть, овладе́ю, овладе́ешь, овладе́л,
    овладе́ла, овладе́ли
16. окра́сить, окра́шу, окра́сишь, окра́сил,
    окра́сила, окра́сили
17. отгры́зть, отгрызу́, отгрызёшь, отгры́з,
    отгры́зла, отгры́зли
18. отли́ть, отолью́, отольёшь, о́тлил, отлила́,
    о́тлили
19. отозва́ть, отзову́, отзовёшь, отозва́л,
    отозвала́, отозва́ли
20. переби́ть, перебью́, перебьёшь, переби́л,
    переби́ла, переби́ли
21. подве́ргнуть, подве́ргну, подве́ргнешь,
    подве́рг, подве́ргла, подве́ргли
22. поддержа́ть, поддержу́, подде́ржишь,
    поддержа́л, поддержа́ла, поддержа́ли.
23. подчеркну́ть, подчеркну́, подчеркнёшь,
    подчеркну́л, подчеркну́ла, подчеркну́ли.

24. претерпе́ть, претерплю́, прете́рпишь,
    претерпе́л, претерпе́ла, претерпе́ли
25. привле́чь, привлеку́, привлечёшь, привлёк,
    привлекла́, привлекли́
26. примежева́ть, примежу́ю, примежу́ешь,
    примежева́л, примежева́ла, примежева́ли
27. приплести́, приплету́, приплетёшь,
    приплёл, приплела́, приплели́
28. присво́ить, присво́ю, присво́ишь, присво́ил,
    присво́ила, присво́или
29. прожи́ть, проживу́, проживёшь, про́жил,
    прожила́, про́жили
30. прорва́ть, прорву́, прорвёшь, прорва́л,
    прорвала́, прорва́ли
31. простоя́ть, просто́ю, простои́шь, простоя́л,
    простоя́ла, простоя́ли
32. простуди́ть, простужу́, просту́дишь,
    простуди́л, простуди́ла, простуди́ли
33. разверну́ть, разверну́, развернёшь,
    разверну́л, разверну́ла, разверну́ли
34. разви́ть, разовью́, разовьёшь, разви́л,
    развила́, разви́ли
35. развороти́ть, разворочу́, разворо́тишь,
    развороти́л, развороти́ла, развороти́ли
36. разгляде́ть, разгляжу́, разгляди́шь,
    разгляде́л, разгляде́ла, разгляде́ли
37. рассова́ть, рассу́ю, рассу́ешь, рассова́л,
    рассова́ла, рассова́ли
38. растолкова́ть, растолку́ю, растолку́ешь,
    растолкова́л, растолкова́ла, растолкова́ли
39. сжать, сожму́, сожмёшь, сжал, сжа́ла,
    сжа́ли
40. сжечь, сожгу́, сожжёшь, сжёг, сожгла́,
    сожгли́
41. сни́зить, сни́жу, сни́зишь, сни́зил, сни́зила,
    сни́зили
42. стере́ть, сотру́, сотрёшь, стёр, стёрла,
    стёрли
43. упа́сть, упаду́, упадёшь, упа́л, упа́ла,
    упа́ли
44. упря́чь, упрягу́, упряжёшь, упря́г, упрягла́,
    упрягли́
45. установи́ть, установлю́, устано́вишь,
    установи́л, установи́ла, установи́ли

EXERCISE

Some of the words listed below imply more than one base form, others only one. Give all the possible base forms implied by each word.

A. *Nonpast tense forms*

1. плывёт
2. засты́ну
3. разу́ют
4. обретёшь
5. стрижём
6. гла́жу
7. торчи́т
8. бре́шете
9. стригу́т
10. блюёт
11. волочу́
12. волочёшь
13. пишу́
14. лгу́т
15. слу́шаю
16. де́ржит
17. па́дает
18. доста́нет
19. уколю́
20. замнёте

B. *Past tense forms*

1. храпе́ла
2. замёрз
3. прибе́гла
4. кра́ли
5. трясло́
6. скры́ла
7. подстри́г
8. схвати́ла
9. сказа́ла
10. вздохну́ли
11. веле́ла
12. принесла́
13. зва́ли
14. запреща́л
15. драла́
16. сдвига́ла
17. ла́яли
18. коро́бил
19. перепо́лнила
20. начала́

C. *Infinitive forms*

1. подры́ть
2. нажа́ть
3. затро́нуть
4. отвести́
5. сия́ть
6. запи́сывать
7. чита́ть
8. испе́чь
9. зале́зть
10. говори́ть
11. уплы́ть
12. подкова́ть
13. держа́ть
14. ползти́

D. *Imperative forms*

1. купи́
2. живи́
3. взгляни́
4. узна́й
5. ста́нь
6. отожни́
7. ду́й
8. зажги́
9. допе́й
10. пла́чь
11. служи́
12. чи́сти
13. веди́
14. пой

EXERCISE (cont.)

C. *Infinitive forms*	D. *Imperative forms*
15. признáть	15. вóй
16. забúть	16. молчú
17. напоúть	17. сóхни
18. свéргнуть	18. нарéжь
19. замáзать	19. снимú
20. терпéть	20. продавáй

QUESTIONS FOR REVIEW

1. Explain the difference between primary and secondary verbs.

2. What division is made of primary verbs? Upon what is this division based?

3. What is meant by a stable environment? Unstable?

4. What may (and may not) happen in each one?

5. In what kinds of verbs is nonpast tense stress shift possible?

6. Why do suffixed verbs not have stress shift in the past tense?

7. What is V+V mutation? How does it differ from the mutation that we see in the nonpast tense of velar obstruent primary stems?

8. What is the most common infinitive ending?

9. In what kinds of verbs do we find some other ending?

10. What is the relationship between the nonpast tense stress pattern and the formation (and place of stress) of the imperative?

CHAPTER SEVEN

VERBAL ADJECTIVES AND VERBAL ADVERBS

There are in Russian four verbal adjectives and two verbal adverbs:

Verbal adjectives	Verbal adverbs
present active	imperfective
present passive	perfective
past active	
past passive	

The present verbal adjectives and the imperfective verbal adverb are formed only from imperfective verbs, while the past passive verbal adjective and the perfective verbal adverb are formed only from perfective verbs.[1] Only the past active verbal adjective is regularly formed from both imperfective and perfective verbs. The passive verbal adjectives are generally formed only from transitive verbs and are the only verbal adjectives that have short (predicate) forms. The suffixed particle is always −ся with verbal adjectives and −сь with verbal adverbs.

To generate the verbal adjectives and verbal adverbs, a formant is added to the base form. When this is done, all of the rules noted in Chapter 6 regarding the combination of base forms and endings will apply. That is, not only are the basic rules of combination relevant, but also the V+V mutation rules, plus any comments about special alternations which were made in the verb type analysis (e.g., $o \rightarrow i$ in OJ verbs, the loss of i in IJ verbs, the insertion of a vowel in certain ns-A verbs, etc.).

---

[1] Occasionally a past passive verbal adjective or a perfective verbal adverb will be formed from an imperfective verb, but such instances are not common.

PRESENT ACTIVE VERBAL ADJECTIVE

There are two formants:

(1) $-u\check{s}\check{c}-$ for all first conjugation verbs;

(2) $-a\check{s}\check{c}-$ for all second conjugation verbs.

These formants are added to the base form and followed by the regular adjective endings (see p. 46.).

PRESENT PASSIVE VERBAL ADJECTIVE

There are two formants:

(1) $-om-$ for all first conjugation verbs;

(2) $-im-$ for all second conjugation verbs.

These formants are added to the base form and followed by the regular adjective endings.[1] This verbal adjective is regularly formed only from *AJ*, *VAJ*, *OVA*, *I*, *E*, and *h-A* verbs.

IMPERFECTIVE VERBAL ADVERB

There is one formant, $-a$, which is added to the base form.[1] As in the imperative (see Rule 2, p. 101), any change in the stem which occurs *throughout* the non-past tense must occur here. This verbal adverb is not generally formed from:

resonant primary stems (except *V* verbs);
ns-A verbs;
velar obstruent stems;
A verbs with stems in *s* or *z*;
NU or *(NU)* verbs.

---

[1]*VAJ* verbs, in forming their present passive verbal adjective and imperfective verbal adverb, add the formant directly to the base form with no loss of *-va-* (e.g., даваемый, давая). Compare the imperative formation of these verbs (Item 1,b on p. 102).

STRESS COMMENTS

Verbs which have stress fixed on a syllable of the stem in the nonpast tense will also have stress on that syllable in the three forms just discussed. All other verbs will have stress on the vowel of the formant. The following exceptions to the stress rule should be noted:

In the present active verbal adjective, stress will retract one syllable in:

(1) all first conjugation verbs with shifting nonpast tense stress (e.g., $p_{\!,}is\text{-}\overset{x}{a}\text{+}$ has пи́шущий);

(2) the following second conjugation verbs:

dav̦-ǐ+	l̦eč-ǐ+	tašč-ǐ+
duš-ǐ+	l̦ub̦-ǐ+	țerp̦-ě+
diš-ǎ+	rub̦-ǐ+	tuš-ǐ+
žen̦-ǐ+	služ-ǐ+	xval̦-ǐ+

EXAMPLES

Base form	Pr act v adj	Pr pas v adj	Imp v adv
plǐv+	плыву́щий		плывя́
nój+	но́ющий		
v̦oz̦+	везу́щий		везя́
str̦ig+	стригу́щий		
max-ǎ+	ма́шущий		маша́
rv-ǎ+	рву́щий		
prob-ova+	про́бующий	про́буемый	про́буя
por-ǒ+	по́рющий		поря́

EXAMPLES (cont.)   •

Base form	*Pr act v adj*	*Pr pas v adj*	*Imp v adv*
ţaǥ-nǔ+	тя́нущий		
ŗeš-àj+	реша́ющий	реша́емый	реша́я
da-vàj+	даю́щий	дава́емый	дава́я
suḑ-ǐ+	судя́щий	суди́мый	судя́
ţerṗ-ě+	те́рпящий	терпи́мый	терпя́
ḑerž-ǎ+	держа́щий	держи́мый	держа́
sòx-(nu)+	со́хнущий		

EXERCISE

Generate present active and present passive verbal adjectives (masculine singular, nominative), and imperfective verbal adverbs, for each of the twenty-five hypothetical verbs on p. 100. Do not generate forms for those verb types that do not regularly admit them.

PAST ACTIVE VERBAL ADJECTIVE

There is one formant, -*vš*-, added to the base form and followed by the regular adjective endings. The *v* of the formant truncates (leaving -*š*-) in obstruent primary stems, resonants of the *R* type, and in *(NU)* verbs.[1] In verbs of the *D/T* type, in the syllable preceding the truncated variant of the formant, the vowel ̦*o* may become ̦*e* (e.g., *pŗi-ұod+* has приве́дший). A very few

---

[1] Certain *(NU)* verbs admit two forms, one without -*nu*-, the other with it. As might be expected, in these instances the full formant (-*vš*-) is added to the vocalic stem (i.e., the one with -*nu*-), while the truncated formant (-*š*-) is added to the consonantal one. For example, from the verb *za-mólk-(nu)+* may be found either замо́лкший or замо́лкнувший.

verbs of this type ($k\overset{\prime}{l}ad+$, $kr\acute{a}d+$, $p\acute{a}d+$, $\underset{\cdot}{s}\acute{e}d+$) exhibit
truncation of the obstruent, rather than of v.[1]

STRESS COMMENTS

Stress in the past active verbal adjective almost
always falls on that syllable which is stressed in the
past tense masculine form. The only exceptions to this
are found among certain verbs with stress on the prefix
in the past masculine form. Such verbs generally do not
have prefixal stress in the past active verbal adjective, but have stress instead on the vowel of the root
(e.g., на́чал but нача́вший, про́жил but прожи́в-
ший, etc.). Among R type verbs, however, stress may
remain on the prefix (за́перший, о́тперший, etc.).

PERFECTIVE VERBAL ADVERB

There is one formant, $-v\check{s}i$. In generating this
form, the same rules noted for forming the past active
verbal adjective will be applied here regarding the loss
or retention of v. Note that when v is retained, the
rest of the formant ($-\check{s}i$) may, and usually does, trun-
cate. Before the suffixed particle $-$сь, however, $-\check{s}i$
must be retained.

Most nonvelar obstruent primary stems generate the
perfective verbal adverb not with the formant $-v\check{s}i$, but
with the imperfective formant $-a$. For example, u-$\eta o\acute{s}+$,
$p\underset{\cdot}{r}i$-$\underset{\cdot}{u}o\acute{z}+$, and za-$b\underset{\cdot}{r}od+$ have унеся́, привезя́, and за-
бредя́.

---

[1]This type of formation, which was originally limited in the literary language to those verbs which were
noted above, now appears among many of the other D/T
verbs as an optional formation. This has resulted in
a series of doublets ($-$бре́дший/$-$бре́вший, $-$ре́тший/
$-$ре́вший, $-$плётший/$-$плёвший). It should be noted
in this connection that the change of $\underset{\cdot}{o}$ to $\underset{\cdot}{e}$ which was
discussed earlier occurs only before the truncated for-
mant (i.e., забрёвший but забре́дший).

From certain verbs in *(NU)* and *R* one occasionally finds variant forms derived from the infinitive stem and using the formant *-v*, rather than *-ši* (e.g., from *zǎ-pr+* and *za-mólk-(nu)+* we have both зáперши and заперéв, замóлкши and замóлкнув).

STRESS COMMENTS

Stress in the perfective verbal adverb is general- ly the same as that of the past active verbal adjective.

EXAMPLES

Base form	*Past act v adj*	*Perf v adv*
do-strój-i+	дострóивший	дострóив
pod-str̨ig+	подстрѝгший	подстрѝгши
za-bol̨-éj+	заболéвший	заболéв
pod-kov-á+	подковáвший	подковáв
za-krój+	закрѝвший	закрѝв
pod-por-ŏ+	подпорóвший	подпорóв
pro-žr-ǎ+	прожрáвший	прожрáв
ot-vǫd+	отвéдший	отведя́ (отвéдши)
ot-bros̨-i+	отбрóсивший	отбрóсив
ot-dox-nu+	отдохнýвший	отдохнýв
na-diš-ǎ+	надышáвший	надышáв
za-maz-a+	замáзавший	замáзав
raz-új+	разýвший	разýв
pr̨i-dum-aj+	придýмавший	придýмав
u-pad+	упáвший	упáв

EXAMPLES (cont.)

Base form	Past act v adj	Perf v adv
raz-den+	раздéвший	раздéв
na-žm+	нажáвший	нажáв
ot-šl̦if-ova+	отшлифовáвший	отшлифовáв
za-verț-ě+	завертéвший	завертéв
za-šij+	зашúвший	зашúв
u-pliv+	уплы́вший	уплы́в
u-krad+	укрáвший	укрáв
za-țix-(nu)+	затúхший/ затúхнувший	затúхши/ затúхнув
ot-pr+	óтперший	óтперши/ отперéв

EXERCISES

    1. Generate a past active verbal adjective and a
perfective verbal adverb for each of the twenty-five hypothetical verbs on p. 100.
    (For this exercise use only the perfective verbs.)

    2. Generate a past active verbal adjective and a
perfective verbal adverb from each of the base forms
which you provided for the verbs on pp. 104-05.

PAST PASSIVE VERBAL ADJECTIVE

There are three formants to which are added the regular adjective endings. When these endings are added to generate the long (attributive) form, the n of the formants -*on*- and -*n*- is doubled. The distribution of these formants is as follows:

(1) -*t*-   all resonant primary stems;
          stems in *NU* and *(NU)*;
          stems in *O*.

(2) -*on*- all obstruent primary stems;
          stems in *I* and *E*.

(3) -*n*-   all other stems.

FORMATION

1. -*t*-. Before this formant the final consonant of syllabic resonant primary stems simply truncates (∅+C), while in nonsyllabic stems the expected changes (*m/n* to ͵*a*; *r* to ͵*or*) occur before the consonant *t*.

2. -*on*-. When this formant is added to obstruent stems, only the expected softening of nonvelar consonants occurs, while in velar stems we find the change of *g/k* to *ž/č* (noted in the verb type analysis as occurring before the vowel *o*).

With regard to the secondary verbs which take the formant -*on*-, V+V mutation occurs regularly in *I* stems and occasionally in *E* stems.

3. -*n*-. The addition of this formant to base forms is unproblematical, and no special comment is needed.

STRESS COMMENTS (LONG FORM)

When the formant -*t*- or -*n*- is added to secondary base forms, stress will retract one syllable if it is on the suffix in the base form. If it is not, then the stress simply remains on that syllable over which the stress mark appears in the base form.

When the formant *-on-* is added to secondary stems,
stress will retract one syllable if the stress pattern
of the nonpast tense is shifting. If stress is fixed,
then the stress will fall on that syllable over which
the stress mark appears in the base form.

When the formant *-t-* is added to resonant primary
stems, and when *-on-* is added to obstruent primary
stems, the tendency is for stress to fall on that syllable which is stressed in the past tense, i.e., to follow
the pattern of stress indicated by the stress symbol in
the base form. For verbs with shifting past tense
stress, this means the place of stress in the nonfeminine forms.

STRESS COMMENTS (SHORT FORM)

For secondary verbs with the formant *-t-* or *-n-*,
the place of stress in the short forms is always the
same as that of the long forms. For other verbs, however, the following additional notations must be made.

Stress on the vowel of the formant *-on-* in the
long forms implies stress on the endings in the short
forms. This is true for both primary and secondary
stems. For primary stems with the formant *-t-*, stress
in the short forms follows the pattern of the past
tense. That is, stress shift in the past tense forms
implies a similar shift in the short forms of the past
passive verbal adjective.

EXAMPLES

Past passive verbal adjective

Base form	Long form	Short forms
s-v̨érg-(nu)+	свéргнутый	свéргнут, —а, —о, —ы
do-strój-i+	дострóенный	дострóен, —а, —о, —ы
za-r̨éz-a+	зарéзанный	зарéзан, —а, —о, —ы
za-str̨íg+	застрúженный	застрúжен, —а, —о, —ы
pod-kov-á+	подкóванный	подкóван, —а, —о, —ы

EXAMPLES (cont.)

Past passive verbal adjective

Base form	*Long form*	*Short forms*
ot-rój+	отры́тый	отры́т, -а, -о, -ы
pod-por-ŏ+	подпо́ротый	подпо́рот, -а, -о, -ы
na-rv-ắ+	на́рванный	на́рван, -а, -о, -ы
ot-v̨od+	отведённый	отведён, -а́, -о́, -ы́
ot-bros̨-i+	отбро́шенный	отбро́шен, -а, -о, -ы
o-ḑen+	оде́тый	оде́т, -а, -о, -ы
za-pak-ovà+	запако́ванный	запако́ван, -а, -о, -ы
u-kràd+	укра́денный	укра́ден, -а, -о, -ы
za-pros̨-ĭ+	запро́шенный	запро́шен, -а, -о, -ы
nă-čn+	на́чатый	на́чат, -а́, -о, -ы
za-pruḑ-i+	запружённый	запружён, -а́, -о́, -ы́
s-tŕ+	стёртый	стёрт, -а, -о, -ы
u-vḷok+	увлечённый	увлечён, -а́, -о́, -ы́
ză-pr+	за́пертый	за́перт, -а́, -о, -ы
za-v̨ert̨-ě+	заве́рченный	заве́рчен, -а, -о, -ы
prŏ-ḷij+	про́литый	про́лит, -а́, -о, -ы
ob-dùm-aj+	обду́манный	обду́ман, -а, -о, -ы
ŏt-ņm+	о́тнятый	о́тнят, -а́, -о, -ы
u-v̨iḑ-e+	уви́денный	уви́ден, -а, -о, -ы
na-žm+	нажа́тый	нажа́т, -а, -о, -ы
pod-žg+	подожжённый	подожжён, -а́, -о́, -ы́

EXERCISES

1. Answer the following questions on the verbs
which were used as examples on the preceding two pages:

a. In which verbs do you find C+V? V+C?
b. In which verbs do you find C+C? In which of
these does something other than simple truncation occur?
Explain what happens in each one.
c. In which verbs do you find V+V? In which of
these does V+V mutation occur? Why does it not occur in
all of them?
d. In which verbs do you find automatic softening
of a paired consonant before 0? In which ones do you
find regular velar mutation before 0?
e. In which verbs does the stress retract one
syllable from the suffix?
f. In which verbs do you find end stress in the
short forms? What do all those verbs have in common?
g. In which verbs do you find stress on the prefix? What do all those verbs have in common?
h. In which verbs does stress remain on the same
syllable over which the stress mark appears in the base
form? What do all those verbs have in common?

2. For each of the twenty-five hypothetical verbs
on p. 100, generate the following forms of the past passive verbal adjective: (1) masculine nominative singular, long form; (2) all short forms. (Remember to use
the perfective aspect of each verb.)

3. Do the same thing for each of the verbs in the
exercise on pp. 104-05.

4. Using the nonprefixed hypothetical base forms
on the following page you are to derive the:

1) first singular nonpast
2) third singular nonpast
3) third plural nonpast
4) imperative
5) present active verbal adjective
6) present passive verbal adjective
7) imperfective verbal adverb

EXERCISES (cont.)

   5. Using the prefixed hypothetical base forms below you are to derive the following forms:

        1) infinitive
        2) past tense, all forms
        3) past active verbal adjective
        4) perfective verbal adverb
        5) past passive verbal adjective, long form
        6) past passive verbal adjective, all short
            forms

1. pḽeț-ě̌+ /u-   14. gr̦én+ /za-

2. m̦es-ǎ̃+ /pod-   15. sák-(nu)+ /do-

3. sp̦ik-ová+ /za-   16. țǐj+ /vz-

4. vḽóg+ /na-   17. blak-áj+ /s-

5. trój+ /raz-   18. zn+ /nad-

6. motr̦-éj+ /u-   19. loț-ǐ+ /pod-

7. zr+ /pŏd-   20. rg+ /ot-

8. lag-ǎ+ /pro-   21. grot̸-nǔ+ /za-

9. br̦ot+ /v-   22. r̦éz+ /pr̦i-

10. gr-ǎ+ /ot-   23. vor-ŏ+ /u-

11. klój-i+ /raz-   24. šiv+ /nǎ-

12. voš-ǎ+ /p̦er̦e-   25. tav̦-ǐ+ /pro-

13. pr̦ov-á+ /pod-

   6. If you were asked to generate the nonpast
tense of the *prefixed* verbs above, in which of them
would the vowel *o* be inserted after the prefix? In
which of them would *o* be inserted in forming the imperative? Explain.

CHAPTER EIGHT

IMPERFECTIVE DERIVATION

With very few exceptions the addition of a prefix to a nonprefixed stem results in the formation of a perfective verb. In some instances the addition of the prefix serves only to create a perfective partner with no change in meaning other than the grammatical one of perfectivization (e.g., *p̧is-å̃+/na-p̧is-å̃+*, *ḑél-aj+/s-ḑél-aj+*, etc.). For the most part, however, the addition of a prefix both changes the meaning of the stem and perfectivizes it as well (e.g., *s-p̧is-å̃+* or *pod-ḑél-aj+*). Such verbs are said to be semantically prefixed.

The derivation of the imperfective aspect from semantically prefixed perfective stems can be seen to follow certain patterns. There are three suffixes by means of which the base form of a semantically prefixed perfective verb may be extended in order to form the corresponding imperfective verb. These suffixes are:

(1) *-áj+*   (2) *-váj+*   (3) *'-ivaj+*

For all three the stress of the resulting verbal stem is defined by the particular suffix, being always on the *a* of *-aj+* and *-vaj+*, and on the vowel of the root in *-ivaj+*. Moreover, it is important to note that although there are three imperfectivizing suffixes, all three create verbs of the same type, namely *AJ*.

The distribution of the suffixes is as follows:

(1) *-aj+* is the suffix for

    (a) *all* nonsyllabic stems;[1]
    (b) obstruent primary stems;
    (c) stems in *(NU)*.

---

[1]A nonsyllabic stem is any stem (primary or secondary) that contains a nonsyllabic root.

(2)   *-vaj+* is the suffix for

(a)   syllabic resonant primary stems;
(b)   stems in *EJ*.

(3)   *-ivaj+* is the suffix for all other stems, but
note that verbs in *I* may have either *-aj+* or
-ivaj+, and verbs in *E* may have any one of
the three. [1]

In addition to the basic rules of combination
noted on p. 79, the following changes are expected to
occur in imperfective derivation:

1.   V+V mutation occurs regularly in *I* verbs before *-aj+* or *-ivaj+* and in certain *E* verbs before
-ivaj+. [2]

2.   Stems in *AJ*, *NU*, and *(NU)* have truncation of
this entire suffix, the imperfectivizing suffix being
added directly to the root.

3.   The vowel *i* is inserted before the final consonant of the root in all nonsyllabic stems. This *i* is
spelled ы everywhere except before *r* and *n*, or where the
spelling rules require the letter и (i.e., after velars,
hushers, or soft paired consonants).

4.   In the syllable preceding the suffix *-ivaj+*, a
root *o* (which is spelled о and is not part of the *ov/uj*
alternation) becomes *a*. [3]

---

[1]Verbs in *I* with a root ending in *j* always take
-ivaj+, while those in *I* of Church Slavic origin regularly take *-aj+*. For the majority of verbs in *I* or *E*,
however, the imperfectivizing suffix must be specified.
    [2]See B,2,b,1) on pp. 131-32 for a list of those
verbs in which the expected mutation does not occur.
See also C,1 on pp. 132-34 for a description of the situation in *E* verbs.
    [3]In about seventy *I* verbs this expected change of
o to *a* does not occur, and about six verbs have variant
imperfective forms, one with *o*, the other with *a*. For
details, see Item C,5,a on pp. 136-37.

A NOTE ON PREFIXATION

When a prefix ending in (or consisting of) a consonant is added to a nonsyllabic root (or a root which
begins with certain consonant clusters), the fill vowel
o (always spelled O) is inserted between the prefix and
the first consonant of the root. When, however, as part
of a regular alternation, another vowel appears in this
root (e.g., the o which appears in the nonpast tense of
certain ns-A verbs, or the i which is inserted in the
imperfective of nonsyllabic verbs), then the fill vowel
is not inserted after the prefix. For example, in add-
ing the prefix ot- to the base form zv-$\overset{\times}{a}$+, a fill vowel
is inserted in the infinitive and past tense forms, but
not in the nonpast tense or in the derived imperfective
(ОТОЗВА́ТЬ and ОТОЗВА́Л, but ОТЗОВУ́ and ОТЗЫВА́ТЬ).

EXAMPLES OF IMPERFECTIVE DERIVATION

The suffix -aj+

(a)   nonsyllabic stems (C+V; insertion of i)

za-tk-nú+   za-tik-áj+

na-žm+   na-žim-áj+

pŏ-ŋm+   po-ŋim-áj+

ob-žg+   ob-žig-áj+

pod-br-ẵ+   pod-ḫir-áj+

za-gβ-nú+   za-gib-áj+

(b)   obstruent primary stems (C+V)

ot-şek+   ot-şek-áj+

u-pád+   u-pad-áj+

pod-str̥íg+   pod-str̥ig-áj+

za-polž+   za-polz-áj+

(c)   stems in *(NU)*   (C+V, entire suffix truncates)

  pro-ņík-(nu)+   pro-ņik-áj+

  ot-vérg-(nu)+   ot-verg-áj+

(d)   stems in *I*   (∅+V. Mutation, where possible.)

  ot-véţ-i+   ot-več-áj+

  ob-nov-í+   ob-novļ-áj+

  iz-viņ-í+   iz-viņ-áj+

  pro-dólž-i+   pro-dolž-áj+

The suffix *-vaj+*

(a)   syllabic resonant primary stems   (∅+C)

  za-ḑén+   za-ḑe-váj+

  pro-dúj+   pro-du-váj+

  ot-plĭv+   ot-pli-váj+

  dŏ-ņij+   do-ņi-váj+

  ot-rój+   ot-ri-váj+ *(o → i)*

(b)   stems in *EJ*   (∅+C)

  za-bоļ-éj+   za-boļ-e-váj+

  o-vlaḑ-éj+   o-vlaḑ-e-váj+

(c)   stems in *E*   (V+C)

  pŗe-ţerņ-ĕ+   pŗe-ţerņ-e-váj+

  za-boļ-é+   za-boļ-e-váj+

The suffix -*ivaj+*

(a) Y̵+V. Mutation in *I* verbs, where possible.

do-pros̨-ī̆+   do-praš-ivaj+ (*o* → *a*)

ot-plat-ī̆+   ot-plač-ivaj+

za-služ-ī̆+   za-slúž-ivaj+

do-strój-i+   do-stráj-ivaj+ (*o* → *a*)

za-máz-a+   za-máz-ivaj+

u-d̨erž-ă̆+   u-d̨érž-ivaj+

ot-stoj-á+   ot-stáj-ivaj+ (*o* → *a*)

raz-s̨éj-a+   raz-s̨éj-ivaj+

pod-p̨is-ă̆+   pod-p̨ís-ivaj+

pod-por-ŏ̆+   pod-pár-ivaj+ (*o* → *a*)

ot-šl̨if-ová+   ot-šl̨if-óv-ivaj+

pod-kov-á+   pod-kóv-ivaj+

(b) C+V (entire suffix truncates)

pr̨i-dúm-aj+   pr̨i-dúm-ivaj+

vz-dróg-nu+   vz-drág-ivaj+ (*o* → *a*)

do-trój̵-nu+   do-trág-ivaj+ (*o* → *a*)

SUMMARY

Nonsyllabic stems have -*aj+* with inserted *i*. Primary stems have either -*aj+* or -*vaj+* (the latter for syllabic resonant stems, the former for all others). The majority of syllabic secondary stems have -*ivaj+*, except that stems in *(NU)* take -*aj+*, stems in *EJ* take -*vaj+*, *I* verbs may use -*aj+* or -*ivaj+*, and stems in *E* may have any of the three.

EXERCISES

1.   Generate an imperfective verb for each of the base forms (ignore Nos. 17 and 26) in the exercise on pp. 89-90.

2.   Do the same for Nos. 1-26 on p. 96.

3.   You may assume that the prefix following each of the twenty-five hypothetical verbs on p. 100 is used to form a semantically prefixed perfective. Derive the imperfective of each one.

4.   Do the same for the hypothetical verbs on p. 119.

SOME COMMENTS ON THE VOWEL *o*

1.   THE ALTERNATION OF *o* AND *e*. There are three instances in conjugation where a root vowel undergoes a change of *o* to *e*. This *o* may be part of the root, or it may be a fill vowel (see Item c, p. 88), but in either case we are dealing with an *o* that is always spelled with a vowel letter from Group II (i.e., ё/e). This alternation occurs in the following environments:

a.   In the infinitive of obstruent primary stems:

ţok+   *has infinitive*   течь   (cf. тёк)

beŗog+   "   беречь (cf. берёг)

u-čt+   "   учесть (cf. учёл)

za-žg+   "   зажечь (cf. зажёг)

b.   In the nonpast tense of the following *A* type verbs:

dŗom-ǎ+   *has 3rd plural*   дремлют

kļop-ǎ+   "   клеплют

 țos-ǎ+   *has 3rd plural*   тѐшут

țrop-ǎ+   "   трѐплют

xḷost-ǎ+   "   хлѐщут

čos-ǎ+   "   чѐшут

šopt-ǎ+   "   шѐпчут

In these verbs, forms with stressed *o* appear
in only the past passive verbal adjective and the
derived imperfective. For example, from the verbs
za-kḷop-ǎ+ and *pṛi-čos-ǎ+* we find заклѐпан, за-
клѐпывать and причѐсан, причѐсывать.

c. In the past active verbal adjective and
perfective verbal adverb of certain obstruent primary stems in *D/T* (see pp. 111-12):

pṛi-ʋod+   привѐдший, привѐдши

iz-ob-ṛot+   изобрѐтший, изобрѐтши

za-bṛod+   забрѐдший, забрѐдши

Note, however, that three stems (*mot+, plot+,
-čt+*) do not have this change of *o* to *e* (мѐтший,
плѐтший, счѐтший, etc.).

2. THE FILL VOWEL. As has been pointed out in
Item 1, above, the fill vowel that appears in the two
stems -*čt+* and *žg+*, whether *o* or *e*, is spelled with a
vowel letter from Group II (ё/е). However, the fill vowel that is inserted after a consonantal prefix (p. 122)
is spelled with a vowel letter from Group I (о). For example:

учѐсть, учёл   отозва́ть

зажѐчь, зажёг   but   подорва́л

                        разольёт

3. THE SPELLING OF *O* AFTER THE CONSONANT *c*. In
the few *OVA* type verbs with a root ending in *c*, the *o* of
the suffix is spelled either e or O depending upon the
place of stress.[1] That is, in all of these verbs the
stress in the base form falls not on the *o* of the suffix, but on the *a*, and in any form of the verb with
stress on that syllable the *O* of the suffix is spelled
e. For example:

pro-tanc-ová+	протанцева́ть, протанцева́л
ot-lupc-ová+	отлупцева́ть, отлупцева́л
za-torc-ová+	заторцева́ть, заторцева́л
ob-ḷic-ová+	облицева́ть, облицева́л
o-koḷc-ová+	окольцева́ть, окольцева́л

However, when stress falls on the *o* of the suffix,
as it does in the past passive verbal adjective and in a
derived imperfective, then this vowel is spelled with
the letter O:

pro-tanc-ová+	протанцо́ван, протанцо́вывать
ot-lupc-ová+	отлупцо́ван, отлупцо́вывать
za-torc-ová+	заторцо́ван, заторцо́вывать
ob-ḷic-ová+	облицо́ван, облицо́вывать
o-koḷc-ová+	окольцо́ван, окольцо́вывать

---

[1]Compare a similar situation noted in declension
when endings that begin with *o* are added to stems that
end in *c*. See Item c, p. 8.

IRREGULARITIES IN IMPERFECTIVE DERIVATION

   There are two major types and several minor types
of irregularity that may occur in imperfective derivation. The first major type is the appearance of a suffix other than the expected one, the second is an unpredictable alternation in the root of the derived imperfective.

A.   SUFFIX OTHER THAN EXPECTED ONE

   1.   *-aj+* instead of *-ivaj+* or *-vaj+*

   a.   Three *A* verbs (*-kl̦ík-a+*, *-r̦éz-a+*, *-síp-a+*)
regularly use *-aj+* rather than *-ivaj+*. With *-r̦éz-a+*
doublets using *-ivaj+* are also found. For example:

za-síp-a+	za-sip-áj+
s-kl̦ík-a+	s-kl̦ik-áj+
pod-r̦éz-a+	pod-r̦ez-áj+ (pod-r̦éz-ivaj+)

   b.   The following *NU* verbs use *-aj+* instead of
-ivaj+. Three have changes in the root which are
noted in parentheses:

-dv̦íǧ-nu+	-dv̦ig-áj+
-kl̦ík-nu+	-kl̦ik-áj+
-pr̦ok-nú+	-pr̦ok-áj+
-șag-nú+	-șag-áj+
-toǥ-nŭ+	-top-áj+
po-lix-nú+	po-lix-áj+
u-žas-nú+	u-žas-áj+
u-lib-nú+șa	u-lib-áj+șa
u-xmil̦-nú+sa	u-xmil̦-áj+șa

-dox-nú+ (*o → i*)   -dix-àj+

-kos-nú+ṣa (*o → a*)   -kas-àj+ṣa

voz-kḷik-nu+ (*k → c*)   voz-kḷic-àj+

c. Two verbs use -*aj*+ instead of -*vaj*+:

-kḷа̌n+ (*a → i*)   -kḷin-àj+

-goу̣-éj+ṣa   -govḷ-àj+ṣa

Note the unexpected mutation in -*govḷ-áj+ṣa*.

2. -*ivaj*+ instead of -*vaj*+ or -*aj*+

a. The stem -*zdoroу̣-éj*+ builds imperfectives
with -*ivaj*+ and has mutation as well. For example:

ví-zdoroу̣-ej+   vi-zdoràvḷ-ivaj+

o-zdoroу̣-éj+   o-zdoràvḷ-ivaj+

b. Three obstruent primary stems build imperfectives with -*ivaj*+ instead of -*aj*+:

-volok+   -volák-ivaj+

-kràd+   -kràd-ivaj+

-čt+   -čìt-ivaj+[1]

The last of these uses -*aj*+ with three prefixes:

po-čt+   po-čit-àj+

pṛed-po-čt+   pṛed-po-čit-àj+

s-čt+   s-čit-àj+

---

[1]It might be more accurate to say that -*čìt-ivaj*+
is based on -*čit-áj*+.

3.   -vaj+ instead of -aj+ or -ivaj+

   a. The following nonsyllabic stems have -vaj+
instead of -aj+:

   raz-tl̨-i̧+ (i → e)   raz-tl̨-e-vȧj+

   pro-dl̨-i̧+ (i → e)   pro-dl̨-e-vȧj+

   za-tm̨-i̧+   (i → e)   za-tm̨-e-vȧj+

   The stem -zr̨-é+, which also regularly uses
-vaj+, occasionally has doublets with -aj+:

   pr̨i-zr̨-é+   pr̨i-zr̨-e-vȧj+ (pr̨i-z̧ir-ȧj+)

   b. The following verbs use -vaj+ instead of
-ivaj+, although variants formed with -ivaj+ also
exist:

   -v̧éj-a+   -v̧e-vȧj+ (-v̧éj-ivaj+)

   -şéj-a+   -şe-vȧj+ (-şéj-ivaj+)

   za-ţéj-a+   za-ţe-vȧj+ (za-ţéj-ivaj+)

   u-poj-i̧+ (i → e)   u-poj-e-vȧj+ (u-pȧj-ivaj+)

   Note that the first three verbs above function
as though they were resonant primary stems. That
is, the suffix is ignored, and the final consonant
of the root (j) truncates before -vaj+. In forming
doublets with -ivaj+, however, these same verbs behave regularly.

B. UNPREDICTABLE ALTERNATIONS IN THE ROOT

   1. Change of root vowel and/or final consonant

      za-str̨ȧn+ (a → e)   za-str̨e-vȧj+

      -sȯx-(nu)+ (o → i) -six-ȧj+

      -suȷ̌-nu+ (uj → ov) -sȯv-ivaj+

-pl̩úž-nu+ (*uj → ov*)   -pl̩óv-ivaj+

The following have already been noted under Item
A,1,b, above (p. 129):

-dox-nú+ (*o → i*)   -dix-áj+

-kos-nú+ṣa (*o → a*)   -kas-áj+ṣa

voz-kl̩ík-nu+ (*k → c*)   voz-kl̩ic-áj+

2.   Unpredictable softening or hardening of final
root consonant(s)

a.   Softening

-kovir-nú+   -kovír̥-ivaj+

-nir-nú+   -nír̥-ivaj+

-švir-nú+   -svír̥-ivaj+

-šnir-nú+   -šnír̥-ivaj+

b.   Hardening

1)   In a small group of *I* verbs not only
does the expected mutation fail to occur, but
the final consonant of the root appears either
in its hard variant (in the case of a paired
consonant) or reverts to an original nonpalatal
consonant (in the case of a husher).

-kup̬-ĭ̆+   -kup-áj+

-kuṣ-ĭ̆+   -kus-áj+

-pust̯-ĭ̆+ (*st → sk*)   -pusk-áj+

-rub̬-ĭ̆+   -rub-áj+

-stup̬-ĭ̆+   -stup-áj+

-xvat̯-ĭ̆+   -xvat-áj+

$$-bró\underset{\backsim}{s}-i+ \qquad\qquad -brás-ivaj+$$

$$-kat\underset{\backsim}{-}\check{i}+ \qquad\qquad -kát-ivaj+$$

$$-lom\underset{\backsim}{-}\check{i}+ \qquad\qquad -lám-ivaj+$$

$$-skoč-\check{i}+ \ (\check{c} \rightarrow k) \qquad -skák-ivaj+$$

$$-tašč-\check{i}+ \ (\check{s}\check{c} \rightarrow sk) \quad -tásk-ivaj+$$

2) Two other I stems exhibit hardening of the final root consonant. One $(-n\underset{\backsim}{z}-i+)$, though nonsyllabic, fails to insert i in imperfective derivation; the other $(-póm\underset{\backsim}{n}-i+)$ is historically nonsyllabic and has an inserted vowel. For example:

$$pro-n\underset{\backsim}{z}-i+ \qquad\qquad pro-nz-áj+$$

$$na-póm\underset{\backsim}{n}-i+ \qquad\qquad na-pom\underset{\backsim}{i}n-áj+$$

c. Mutation affecting the penultimate consonant

Two verbs have an unpredictable mutation of the next to last consonant of the root. The first of these also exhibits the $t/\check{s}\check{c}$ alternation noted in Item 2, p. 81:

$$u-m\underset{\backsim}{e}rtv\underset{\backsim}{-}i+ \qquad\qquad u-m\underset{\backsim}{e}rš\check{c}vl\underset{\backsim}{-}áj+$$

$$-mísl\underset{\backsim}{-}i+ \qquad\qquad -mišl\underset{\backsim}{-}áj+$$

C. OTHER TYPES OF IRREGULARITY

1. Stems in E

There are two major problems with E stems, the first relating to the choice of suffix, the second to whether or not mutation occurs.

a. The suffix $-vaj+$

Before the suffix $-vaj+$ no problems occur,

since the verbal suffix -*e* remains, and -*vaj+* is
added directly (V+C):

za-boḷ-é+   za-boḷ-e-vaj+

pṛe-ṭerṇ-ě̃+   pṛe-ṭerṇ-e-vaj+

b.   The suffix -*aj+*

Before -*aj+* the final root consonant appears
in its hard variant:

za-goṛ-é+   za-gor-áj+

pṛi-kip-é+   pṛi-kip-áj+

c.   The suffix -*ivaj+*

Before the suffix -*ivaj+* we find both mutation as well as the lack of it, the latter expectedly accompanied by hardening of the final
consonant of the root:

Mutation

raz-smotṛ-ě̃+   raz-smátṛ-ivaj+

u-ṣid̨-é+   u-ṣiž-ivaj+

vi-ṿerṭ-e+   vi-ṿerč-ivaj+

Hardening

raz-gḷad̨-é+   raz-gḷad-ivaj+

do-ṿerṭ-ě̃+   do-ṿort-ivaj+[1]

---

[1]The alternation *e/o* in this verb requires comment.
When the final root consonant hardens, which in this
verb occurs only in imperfective derivation, the root
vowel changes from *e* to *o*. In addition to the prefix
do-, this occurs with the prefixes *v-*, *s-*, and *na-*. (In
the case of *na-*, both *na-ṿort-ivaj+* and   (*cont.*)

To sum up the situation for verbs in *E* we may say that with the suffix *-vaj+* there are no complications; with the suffix *-aj+* the final root consonant always hardens; and with *-ivaj+* mutation is generally the rule, except for the stems *-gl̦aḑ-é+* (all prefixes) and *-v̦erț-ě̇+* (certain prefixes). When hardening occurs in the latter, the root vowel changes to *o*.

2. Stems in *VAJ*

The three stems in *VAJ* remain imperfective when prefixed and exhibit the following sets of relationships:

Perfective stem	Imperfective stem
-znáj+	-zna-váj+
-dǎj+ [*irreg.*]	-da-váj+
-stán+	-sta-váj+

3. Verbs of motion

It is often stated that the verbs of motion do not follow the same rules of imperfective derivation that nonmotion verbs do, and instead of extending the perfective stem are said to use a second stem (i.e., that of the nondetermined form). This is only partially true, since as many as six of the motion verbs may be seen to derive their imperfectives according to the basic rules of imperfective derivation. They are:

-br̦ód+	-br̦od-áj+
-l̦éz+	-l̦ez-áj+

---

na-v̦érč-ivaj+ exist, but with different meanings.) When mutation occurs with any of the remaining prefixes, however, then no such alternation is expected. Doublets are found with certain prefixes, for example, the verb *per̦e-v̦erț-ě̇+* with both перевéрчивать as well as перевёртывать.

-polz̓+   -polz-a̓j+

-plĭ̓v+   -pli-va̓j+

-kat̬-ĭ̓+   -ka̓t-ivaj+

-tašč-ĭ̓+   -ta̓sk-ivaj+

The hardening in the last two stems above has been noted in B,2,b,1), above. Of the remaining eight motion verbs, six use the unaltered stem of the nondetermined verb in imperfective derivation, while two make a change in that stem. They are:

-jd̓+ [*irreg.*]   -xoɖ-ĭ̓+

-v̬od̓+   -voɖ-ĭ̓+

-v̬oz̓+   -voz̬-ĭ̓+

-n̬os̓+   -nos̬-ĭ̓+

-ḷet̬-e̓+   -ḷet-a̓j+

-gn-ắ+ [*irreg.*]   -gon̬-a̓j+

-je̓x-a+ [*irreg.*]   -jezž-a̓j+   (je̓zɖ-i+)

-ḫež-a̓+ [*irreg.*]   -ḫeg-a̓j+   (ḫe̓g-aj+)

4. Suppletion

    a. The stem -*lož-ĭ̓+* builds imperfectives in one of two ways, neither of which is regular. One possible stem (-*klắd-ivaj+*) presents an example of suppletion, the other (-*lag-a̓j+*) of a change in both root vowel and final consonant. As a general rule, when the same prefix occurs with both imperfective stems, verbs formed with -*lag-a̓j+* tend to have meanings that are either more abstract or more learned than their counterparts with -*klắd-ivaj+*. For example:

    na-lož-ĭ̓+/na-lag-a̓j+   '*impose*' *(a burden,*
                                                    tax, etc.)

na-lož-ı̆+/na-klád-ivaj+   *'load, pack' (a box,*
                                basket, etc.)

ot-lož-ı̆+/ot-lag-áj+   *'deposit' (in geology)*

ot-lož-ı̆+/ot-klád-ivaj+   *'put aside; post-*
                                pone'

   b. The irregular verbs *ḷog̓+* and *şéd+* (лечь,
сесть), which regularly build imperfectives with
-aj+ as expected, also use the stems *-klád-ivaj+* and
-sáž-ivaj+şa, respectively, with certain prefixes.
For example:

pṛi-ḷog̓+   pṛi-ḷog-áj+

ob-şéd+   ob-şed-áj+

But:

u-ḷog̓+şa   u-klád-ivaj+şa

pṛi-şéd+   pṛi-sáž-ivaj+şa

5. Failure to exhibit an expected alternation

   a. A fairly large number[1] of verbs fail to exhibit the *o/a* alternation of the root vowel before
the suffix *-ivaj+*. Several stems, not all of them
common, combine with a number of prefixes:

-xlóp-nu+   -xlóp-ivaj+

---

[1]Although the number of such verbs exceeds 150, the
stylistic level of many of them runs from bookish to ar-
chaic to substandard. A large number of those that are
considered standard literary forms are either uncommon
or highly specialized. A few verbs have doublets whereby forms with *o* and *a* exist side by side in varying
stages of acceptability (обусло́вливать/обусла́вли-
вать, заподо́зривать/заподázривать, сосредо-
то́чивать/сосредота́чивать).

-štóp-aj+   -štóp-ivaj+

-sróč-i+   -sróč-ivaj+

-supóņ-i+   -supóņ-ivaj+

-musól̦-i+   -musól̦-ivaj+

Most of the remaining stems combine with only
one or two prefixes. Some representative examples
are:

raz-tŗevóž-i+   raz-tŗevóž-ivaj+

pŗi-čmók-nu+   pŗi-čmók-ivaj+

pŗi-tóp-nu+   pŗi-tóp-ivaj+

o-ḩez-ból̦-i+   o-ḩez-ból̦-ivaj+

b.   Verbs that fail to exhibit expected mutation
and thus have hardening of the final root consonant
have already been treated in B,2,b and C,1,b and c,
above.

6.   Anomalous alternations

Two verbs are characterized by an anomalous alternation of stems in imperfective derivation. They
are:

raᴢ-í-nu+   raᴢ-e-váj+

ví-nu+   vi-ņim-áj+

The first of these becomes less of an anomaly
when analyzed as *raᴢ-ᴢíj-nu+* and assigned to the group
of verbs noted in Item 3,b on p. 130 which use *-vaj+* instead of *-ivaj+*. Like a few other *NU* verbs (Item B,1 on
pp. 130-31), this one likewise exhibits a change of root
vowel (*i → e*) in deriving its imperfective. The verb
ví-nu+, as can be seen from its imperfective, belonged
originally to the *ŊM* subtype, but its perfective form no
longer contains any indication of this relationship.

CHAPTER NINE

IRREGULARITIES

Although certain irregularities have already been
treated above (irregularities in noun stress in Chapter
2, deviations from the fill vowel rules in Chapters 3
and 4, irregularities in imperfective derivation in
Chapter 8), there remains to be analyzed a number of
nouns and verbs. These irregularities will be treated
in this chapter in one of two ways. In those instances
where a complete listing seems practical, completeness
will be attempted. In other instances, reference will
be made to the Academy grammar, V. V. Vinogradov et al.,
eds., *Grammatika russkogo jazyka*, I (M.: AN SSSR, 1960
[rpt.]), where complete lists of the items in question
can be found. Such references will use the abbreviation
Ak followed by a number indicating the appropriate page
or pages.

IRREGULARITIES IN THE NOUN

A. Nouns ending in -*m̩+a*

There are ten neuter nouns ending in -*m̩+a* that
have the following pattern of declension:

	Singular	*Plural*
N	и́мя	имена́
A	и́мя	имена́
G	и́мени	имён
P	и́мени	имена́х
D	и́мени	имена́м
I	и́менем	имена́ми

The other nine are: бре́мя, вре́мя, вы́мя, зна́-
мя, пла́мя, пле́мя, се́мя, стре́мя, те́мя. All of
these nouns except зна́мя follow the stress pattern outlined above (—ˣ— + —); it too has a shifting pattern,
but the stress in the plural is on the other syllable of
the stem, rather than on the endings (знаме́на, зна-
ме́н, знаме́нах, etc.). The two nouns се́мя and стре́-
мя have a change of o to a in the G pl (семя́н, стре-
мя́н).

B. *Singularia tantum*

There is a large group of nouns that have only
singular forms. Such nouns usually belong to one of
three groups: (1) collective nouns indicating a group
of people or objects viewed as a unit (студе́нчество,
листва́); (2) abstract nouns indicating a quality, an
action, or a concept (геро́йзм, борьба́, о́бщность),
and (3) mass nouns indicating some sort of substance
(са́хар, желе́зо, не́фть). The last named group may
form plurals when the reference is to various kinds of
a substance (кре́пкие табаки́, души́стые чаи́). (See
Ak, 113-15.)

C. *Pluralia tantum*

There is a large group of nouns that have only
plural forms. Nouns in this group usually include
paired or compound items (брю́ки, счёты, очки́) or
items signifying a plural totality of a collective nature (де́ньги, джу́нгли, фина́нсы). The major problem with nouns of this type is that it is not always
possible to predict the ending of the G pl. The following generalizations may serve to eliminate some of this
ambiguity:

(1) If the stem of the noun ends in a soft paired
consonant or a husher, then the G pl ending will be -ej
(гу́сли, гу́слей; щи́, ще́й).

(2) If the stem of the noun ends in j, or if the
ending is stressed -i, then the G pl ending will be -ov
(обби, оббев; весь,́ весо́в; духи́, духо́в).

(3)   If the noun has the ending -*a* in the *N pl*,
then the *G pl* ending will always be -*∅* (дрова́, дрóв;
черни́ла, черни́л).

Thus, it is when such nouns end in unstressed -*i*
preceded by a hard paired consonant or a velar that
there is ambiguity regarding the ending of the *G pl* (either -*∅* or -*ov*). For example: подмо́стки, подмóст-
ков; брю́ки, брю́к; перекóры, перекóров; шаро-
ва́ры, шарова́р. (See *Ak*, 116-18; 174-76.)

D.   Indeclinable nouns

There is a large number of indeclinable nouns,
most of them recent borrowings from other languages.
Such nouns are (1) neuter, if they refer to inanimate
objects (аргó, такси́, клише́, меню́, антраша́); (2)
masculine, if they refer to male human beings or to the
general name for an animal (дéнди, я́нки, шимпанзé,
кенгуру́); or (3) feminine, if they refer to female human beings or unambiguously to the female of the species
(лéди, мада́м, ми́ссис). Exceptions: the noun кóфе
is masculine (according to the reference books, but neuter modifiers are very common in spoken Russian), and
the nouns а́льма ма́тер and берсёз are feminine.
(See *Ak*, 179-80.)

E.   Declension of surnames

1. Russian surnames ending in -*in* and -*ov* (Бул-
га́нин, Морóзов) are declined like pronominal adjectives in the feminine singular and in the plural. The
masculine forms, however, are declined like masculine
nouns ending in -*∅*, except that the *I sg* ending is -*im*
instead of -*om*. For those in -*ov*, stress is always
fixed on the syllable which is stressed in the *N sg*
masc. Those in -*in* also have fixed stress, except that
stress on the suffix -*in* implies end stress in all
forms (Карамзи́н, Карамзина́, Карамзинé, etc.).

2. Surnames that are adjectival in form (Бéлый,
Попла́вский, Трубецкóй) are declined according to
the adjective declension for all forms. The stress, as
in adjectives, is fixed on that syllable which bears the

stress in the *N sg masc.*

3.   Surnames that end in *-ix*, *-ago*, or *-ovo* are
indeclinable (Черны́х, Живáго, Дурновó). So too are
surnames of Ukrainian origin that end in *-enko* and *-ko*.
(Occasionally this latter group may be declined like
feminine nouns in *-a*: Шевчéнко, Шевчéнку, Шевчéн-
ки, etc.) Also not declined are surnames of foreign
origin ending in a vowel (Шóу, Гёте, Гарибáльди,
etc.).

4.   Surnames of either Russian or foreign origin
that end in a consonant (Пастернáк, Ивáск, Шекспи́р,
Брáун, Шми́дт) are declined like masculine nouns in *-Ø*
for the masculine singular forms and the plural forms,
while the feminine forms are not declined at all. Russian surnames that end in *-a* (Гли́нка, Ягóда) are declined like feminine nouns in *-a* whether they refer to a
male or a female.

F.   Plural stem different from singular stem

1.   The affix *-j-*

A number of masculine and neuter nouns add the
affix *-j-* to the stem of the noun when generating the
plural forms. Before this affix hard paired consonants
expectedly soften, *k* goes to *č*, and *g* goes to *z*. In addition, this affix functions like a nonsyllabic ending
with regard to the appearance of a fill vowel. Thus,
from *kam/n̦+Ø* and *d/n+o* we get камéнья and дóнья. The
endings for the *N* and *G pl* for these nouns are *-a* and
-ov, respectively, except that for those with end stress
in the plural *-Ø* replaces *-ov*. When this happens, the
stem ends in consonant plus *j*, a cluster that always requires a fill vowel. Since stress will fall on the fill
vowel, and since *j* is the final element of the cluster,
the fill vowel must be *e* (мужéй, друзéй, князéй).
Note that several of these nouns (those marked [<] below) have a shift of stress not to the endings in the
plural, but to the other syllable of the stem.
The following is a list of those nouns with
the affix *-j-*:

Masculine

brús+∅	kŏr/ņ̣+∅ [<]	strúp+∅
zúb+∅	kṛuk+∅̆̆	stúl+∅
kǎm/ņ̣+∅ [<]	ḷist+∅̆̆	súk+∅
kḷin+∅	loskut+∅̆̆	úgoḷ+∅
klok+∅̆̆	ŏbod+∅ [<]	drŭg+∅
kol+∅̆̆	pŏvod+∅ [<]	kņǎz̧+∅
kŏlos+∅ [<]	pŏloz+∅ [<]	mŭž+∅
kóm+∅	prút+∅	

Neuter

d̦ě̆ṛev+o [<]	koḷén+o	poḷén+o
d/n+ŏ̆	kril+ŏ̆	šíl+o
zv̧en+ŏ̆	ṛer+ŏ̆	

Certain of the nouns listed above have, in addition to the irregularly formed plurals noted here, a set of regular plural forms (see Section H, below). In some instances the regular formation will involve a different stress pattern and, therefore, a different base form. For example, the noun зу́б, when regular, has the base form *zùb+∅*, while with the affix *-j-* it has *zúb+∅*. Therefore, the base forms cited above are valid for a given noun only in combination with the affix *-j-*.

The two nouns *s̆ìn+∅* and *kŭm+∅* have the compound affix *-ov̧-j-* (сыновья́, кумовья́). The latter, though end stressed in the plural has *-ov* for its *G pl* ending instead of *-∅* (кумовьёв, but сынове́й, as expected). Similarly, the nouns *d̆ěv̧eṛ+∅* and *z̧ǎţ+∅* have *-ov* instead of *-∅* in their *G pl* (деверьёв, зятьёв). The noun *s̆uṛin+∅* (which loses the suffix *-in-* in the plural) also has *-ov* in the *G pl* (шурьёв).

2. Other modifications in the stem

a. The suffixes *-aŋ-in-* and *-in-*

All nouns with the suffix *-aŋ-in-* (except
семьянúн), as well as those nouns with the suffix *-in-*
listed below, drop *-in-* in their plural forms. Those
with *-aŋ-in-* all have a *N pl* in *-e* and a *G pl* in *-Ø*;
those with *-in-* likewise have a *G pl* in *-Ø*, but their
N pl is less easily categorized (see list below). If
stress is on the second syllable of the suffix *-aŋ-in-*,
it must retract by one syllable when *-in-* drops (армя-
нúн, армя́не; славянúн, славя́не). (Exception:
гражданúн, гра́ждане, with retraction to the first
syllable.)

ба́рин	ба́ре (ба́ры)
болга́рин	болга́ры
боя́рин	боя́ре
господúн	господа́
тата́рин	тата́ры
хоза́рин	хоза́ры
хозя́ин	хозя́ева
шу́рин	шурья́ (see F,1, above)

b. The suffix *-on/k-*

Nouns with the suffix *-on/k-* (indicating
the young of animals) replace this suffix with *-at-* before the plural endings. The *N pl* has *-a*, the *G pl*, *-Ø*
(*ţelón/k+Ø:* теля́та, теля́т; *galčón/k+Ø:* галча́та,
галча́т). The nouns бесёнок and чертёнок use the
suffix *-oŋ-at-* (бесеня́та, чертеня́та). The noun ще-
нóк (in which the *-on-* is really part of the root) has
doublets in the plural: щеня́та, щеня́т, etc. and
щенкú, щенкóв, etc.

c. Miscellaneous changes

The following nouns have changes in the stem involving (1) mutation, (2) softening, (3) hardening, (4) addition of an affix, (5) loss of a suffix, or (6) suppletion:

	N sg	*Plural forms*
(1)	о́ко	о́чи, оче́й
	у́хо	у́ши, уше́й
(2)	коле́но	коле́ни, коле́ней
	сосе́д	сосе́ди, сосе́дей
	чёрт	че́рти, черте́й
(3)	це́рковь	це́ркви, церкве́й, церква́х, церква́м, церква́ми
(4)	не́бо	небеса́, небе́с
	чу́до	чудеса́, чуде́с
(5)	ку́рица	ку́ры, ку́р
	су́дно	суда́, судо́в
	цвето́к	цветы́, цвето́в
(6)	челове́к	лю́ди, люде́й, лю́дях, лю́дям, людьми́
	ребёнок	де́ти, дете́й, де́тях, де́тям, детьми́

Note that in the last two nouns above we also have an irregular stress pattern and irregular *I pl* forms.

G. Irregularities affecting isolated case forms

1. *N* and/or *G pl*

a. Neuter nouns ending in -*k+o* have -*i* in the *N pl* instead of the expected -*a*. If these nouns have end stress in the plural, they will have the ending -*ov* in the *G pl* instead of -*∅*. For example:

Base form	*N pl*	*G pl*
okóš/k+o	окбшки	окбшек
koļéč/k+o	колéчки	колéчек
očk+ó	очки́	очкбв
ušk+ó	ушки́	ушкбв

A few nouns deviate from this pattern. In *ŏblak+o*
and *ŏblačk+o* we find *-a* in the *N pl*, instead of the expected *-i*, but the *G pl* has *-ov* (облакá, облакбв;
облачкá, облачкбв). Conversely, the nouns *ļíčik+o*
and *pļéčik+o* have *-i* as expected in their *N pl*, but in
the *G pl* have *-ov*, even though stress is on the stem
(ли́чики, ли́чиков; плéчики, плéчиков). The noun
vŏjsk+o does not follow this pattern at all and has *-a*
and *-∅* instead of *-i* and *-ov* (войскá, вбйск).

b. A small group of feminine nouns with base
forms that end in consonant plus *-ņ+a* have a loss of
softening of the final consonant of the stem in their
G pl forms. Some common nouns of this type are:

Base form	*G pl*
vļiš/ņ+a	ви́шен
ŗés/ņ+a	пéсен
bàs/ņ+a	бáсен
sòt/ņ+a	сбтен

Three nouns of this type are exceptional in
that they do not have this loss of softening:

deŗèv/ņ+a	деревéнь
bàriš/ņ+a	бáрышень
kùx/ņ+a	кýхонь

c.   Nouns with -∅ instead of -*ov* in the *G pl*

1)   All nouns with the suffix -*in*- which
designate a national or ethnic group (e.g., грузи́н,
мордви́н, осети́н), as well as the small number of similar nouns listed below, have -∅ instead of -*ov* in the
G pl.

абази́н   башки́р   туркме́н

балка́р   буря́т   ту́рок

цыга́н (Note: the *N pl* is цыга́не.)

2)   A number of nouns designating members
of military groups:

гренаде́р   каде́т   партиза́н

гуса́р   кираси́р   солда́т

драгу́н

3)   A small group of nouns often used with
numerals:

арши́н   гра́мм   ра́з

во́льт   гра́н   челове́к

To this group also belongs the noun во́лос
with the *G pl* воло́с.

4)   A number of nouns designating items
often found in pairs:

ва́ленок   погон   чуло́к

гла́з   сапо́г

5)   Diminutives of a number of nouns cited
above (e.g., гла́з, сапо́г) may likewise have a *G pl* in

-∅, while on occasion a noun with a regular *G pl* form
will also exhibit this irregularity (e.g., the last two
nouns listed below):

глазо́к   сапожо́к

зубо́к   рожо́к

   d.   Nouns with -*ej* instead of -∅ in the *G pl*

        A group of nouns ending in soft consonant
or husher plus -*a* has the *G pl* ending -*ej* instead of the
expected -∅:

бахча́	клешня́	ра́спря
броня́	левша́	ро́хля
бу́кля	лю́тня	са́кля
вожжа́	мя́мля	свеча́
головня́	ноздря́	ступня́
долбня́	паша́	тётя
до́ля	пе́ня	тихбня
дя́дя	праща́	ханжа́
западня́	при́горшня	ца́пля
каланча́	пятерня́	ю́ноша
квашня́		

        The two nouns мо́ре, по́ле also belong in
this group (море́й, поле́й).

   2.   Second genitive

        A number of masculine nouns denoting divisible
substances have the ending -*u* (instead of -*a*) in their
G sg when used with expressions of quantity. Some of
the more common ones are:

бензи́н	карто́фель	мёд
виногра́д	ква́с	ме́л
во́здух	клей	пе́рец
во́ск	кумы́с	по́рох
горо́х	ле́с	пу́х
ды́м	лимона́д	ри́с
жи́р	лу́к	сала́т

сáхар	сы́р	цемéнт
снéг	табáк	чáй
сóк	творóг	шёлк
спи́рт	ýксус	шоколáд
сýп	хрéн	я́д

With any other use of the genitive case (object of
a preposition, to indicate possession, etc.) or when
such nouns are modified by an attributive, the regular
ending must be used: без виногрáда, зáпах табакá,
стакáн крéпкого чáя, etc.

There is also a smaller group of more or less abstract nouns that likewise have this ending when there
is some notion of quantification. They are:

блéск	ви́зг	простóр
брáк	жáр	разговóр
вéс	кри́к	свéт
вздóр	лóск	спóр

In addition, there is a small group of nouns that
replace *-a* with *-u* when used with certain prepositions.

With без: вéс, óтдых, разбóр, ри́ск,
                 спрóс, счёт, убы́ток, шýм.

With из: ви́д, дóм, лéс.

With с (meaning 'because of'): гóлод, испýг,
                 перепýг, смéх, стрáх.

There is also a large number of idiomatic expressions in which *-u* replaces *-a*. For example:

с глáзу на глáз	бéз году недéля
не хвати́ло дýху	с ми́ру по ни́тке
сби́ться с тóлку	спóру нéт
не до смéху	покóю нéт
дáть мáху	ни óтдыху, ни срóку
нéт счёту	не давáть спýску
прибáвить шáгу	ни шáгу назáд
с чáсу на чáс	ýдержу нéт

(For a complete list of masculine nouns with a
G sg in *-u*, see *Ak*, 141-43.)

3. Second locative

There is a fairly large group of masculine nouns (mostly monosyllabic) which replace the normal ending of the *P sg* with -*u* (always stressed), when the noun is used as the object of a preposition indicating a concrete sense of location or time. Some of the most common examples are:

а́д	кра́й	по́ст
ба́л	кру́г	по́т
бе́рег	лёд	пу́х
бо́к	ле́с	ра́й
бо́й	ло́б	ро́т
бо́рт	мёд	ря́д
ве́тер	ме́х	са́д
ви́д	мо́ст	снѐг
гла́з	но́с	со́к
го́д	па́р	спи́рт
до́лг	пи́р	стро́й
ды́м	пле́н	ты́л
жа́р	по́л	у́гол
жи́р	по́лк	хо́д
кле́й	по́рт	шка́ф (*Ak*, 143-45)

A much smaller group of feminine nouns has a similar special second locative ending. These are all nouns with a *N sg* ending in -∅ and stress on the stem in the singular. For their second locative form these nouns simply shift the stress to the ending (e.g., о гря́зи, but в грязи́). They are:

го́рсть	кро́вь	сте́пь
гру́дь	но́чь	те́нь
две́рь	пе́чь	це́пь
кле́ть	свя́зь	че́сть
ко́сть	се́ть	(*Ak*, 204-05)

(Note that for the four nouns гру́дь, пе́чь, сте́пь, це́пь, an alternate stress on the ending is possible when these nouns are used as the object of certain prepositions requiring the genitive or dative case. For example: от груди́, по цепи́, по груди́, etc.)

H.   Nouns with two sets of plural forms

There is a large group of nouns for which there exist two *N pl* forms. In some instances it is only the nominative case forms that are involved in this bifurcation, at other times it is the entire set of plural forms, but in either event there is always a distinction in meaning between the two sets of forms.

One group of nouns of this kind involves forms with a *N pl* ending in either -*a* or -*i*:

бо́ров	борова́	'horizontal flues'
	бо́ровы	'hogs
мех	меха́	'furs'
	мехи́	'leather vessels; bellows'
о́браз	образа́	'icons'
	о́бразы	'shapes, forms, images'
о́рден	ордена́	'medals, decorations'
	о́рдены	'orders' (i.e., societies)
по́вод	повода́	'reins'
	по́воды	'causes'
по́яс	пояса́	'belts' (clothing)
	по́ясы	'belts, zones' (geography)
про́вод	провода́	'wires'
	про́воды	'farewell' (no singular)
про́пуск	пропуска́	'passes, permits'
	про́пуски	'absences, gaps'
со́боль	соболя́	'sables' (furs)
	со́боли	'sables' (animals)
счёт	счета́	'bills; accounts'
	счёты	'abacus' (no singular)
тон	тона́	'tones' (painting)
	то́ны	'tones' (music)

тóрмоз	тормозá	'brakes'
	тóрмозы	'obstacles'
хлéб	хлебá	'corn, crops, cereal'
	хлéбы	'loaves' (of bread)
цвéт	цветá	'colors'
	цветы́	'flowers' (*sg:* цветóк)
ю́нкер	юнкерá	'cadets'
	ю́нкеры	'Junkers' (Prussian landowners)

A second group involves the use of regular endings opposed to a second set of endings which include the affix -*j*- (see F,1, above, pp. 141-42):

зу́б	зу́бы	'teeth'
	зу́бья	'cogs'
кáмень	кáмни	'stones'
	камéнья	'stones' (collective)
клóк	клокú	'rags'
	клóчья	'rags' (collective)
кóл	колы́	'*F*'s' (lowest mark in school)
	кóлья	'pickets, stakes'
колéно	колéна	'bends' (of a river)
	колéни	'knees'
	колéнья	'joints' (tech.)
кóрень	кóрни	'roots'
	корéнья	'spices, herbs' (no singular)
крюк	крюкú	'hooks'
	крю́чья	'hooks' (for supporting a load)
лúст	листы́	'sheets' (of paper)
	лúстья	'leaves' (of plants, etc.)
лоскýт	лоскуты́	'rags, scraps'
	лоскýтья	'rags, scraps' (collective)
сы́н	сыны́	'sons' (figuratively)
	сыновья́	'sons'

A third group involves a different place of stress and, in the *G pl*, a different ending:

глазо́к	гла́зки, гла́зок	'eyes' (diminutive)
	глазки́, глазко́в	'eyes, eyelets' (tech.);
		'buds, eyes' (of potato)
зубо́к	зу́бки, зу́бок	'teeth' (diminutive)
	зубки́, зубко́в	'bits' (for drilling)
рожо́к	ро́жки, ро́жек	'horns' (diminutive)
	рожки́, рожко́в	'horns' (music)

I. Miscellaneous irregularities

1. The nouns *dòč̌+∅* [*f*] and *màt̯+∅* [*f*] insert *-er-* before the ending in all forms except the *N* and *A sg*.

2. The noun *put̯+∅́* has the ending *-i* in the *G, P,* and *D sg* instead of the expected *-a*, *-e*, and *-u*, respectively.

3. The noun *pl̯eč̌+ò* has the ending *-i* in the *N pl* instead of the expected *-a*.

4. Four nouns drop the vowel *a* of the *I pl* ending *-ami*: детьми́, дочерьми́, лошадьми́, людьми́. The noun *dv̯er̯+∅* [*f*] has дверьми́ as an alternate to дверя́ми, while both лошадя́ми and дочеря́ми are given alternate status.

5. The noun *gòd+∅* (with the alternate base form *gǒd+∅* [*a*]) uses the genitive plural of *l̯ět+o* with numerals and other quantifiers (во́семь ле́т, мно́го ле́т).

6. The noun Христо́с has the base form *Xr̯ist+∅́* for all forms except the *N sg*.

7. The noun госпо́дь has the base form *gòspod+∅* for all forms except the *N sg*.

8. Two nouns have special vocative forms: бо́г — бо́же, госпо́дь — го́споди.

IRREGULARITIES IN THE VERB

A verb is considered irregular when any form (or forms) of that verb cannot be generated correctly from a base form.   Therefore, for irregular verbs it is neces- sary to make additional notations about those forms of the verb that cannot be generated correctly.

For a small number of irregular verbs these addi- tional notations may be made by means of a second base form.   In such instances the first base form both de- fines the verb type and functions as the base form to be used in imperfective derivation and before *consonantal* endings, while the second base form is to be used when *vocalic* endings are added.   Occasionally it is necessary to include some additional comment regarding stress or the generation of a single form.

The following verbs may be described in terms of two base forms:

1.   ŗev-é+ / ŗev+

2.   bŗíj+ / bŗej+

3.   mol-ŏ+ / ṃel-ŏ+

4.   stl-á+ / stֻel-ă+

5.   gn-ă+ / goṇ-ĭ+

6.   o-př+ / ob-pr+

7.   alk-á+ / álk-a+

8.   koֻleb-á+ / koֻléb-a+

9.   kolix-á+ / kolíx-a+ [*imperative:*   колыхáй]

10.   ֻlog+́ / ֻlag+ [*stem stress in nonpast*]

11.   şéd+ / şad+ [*stem stress in nonpast*]

12.   ֻpéj+ / poj+ [*end stress in nonpast;*
                    imperative: пóй]

13.   jéx-a+ / jed+ [*stem stress in nonpast;*
                    imperative: поезжáй]

14. bĭj+ / bud+ [*stem stress in nonpast; imperfec-*
                    tive verbal adverb: бу́дучи]

    For a second group of verbs it is necessary to de-
scribe the irregularities by means of additional comments, rather than by citing a second base form. They
are:

1. klă̆n+ [*end stress in nonpast;*
              infinitive: клясть]

2. gṇĭj+ [*end stress in nonpast*]

3. raz-pń+ [*fill vowel not inserted:*   распну́,
              распнёшь, распни́, *etc.*]

4. pṛĭ-ṇm+ [ṇ *truncates in nonpast; stress in*
              nonpast is shifting]

5. rast́+ [t *truncates before consonant or* -∅;
              a *becomes* o *in past forms*]

6. id́+ [*infinitive:*   идти́; *stem for all past*
              forms (except past passive verbal adjec-
              tive) is šd+; *when prefixed,* i *becomes* j
              before vocalic endings, and d *truncates*
              in infinitive; prefixes ending in a con-
              sonant insert o *before* шёл]

7. ḷeź+ [*stem stress in nonpast*]

8. moǵ+ [*shifting stress in nonpast*]

9. tolḱ+ [*final consonants behave like nonsyllab-*
              ic root, but fill vowel is o, *not* ̦o]

10. tk-ă̆+ [k *does not mutate before* o, *it softens*]

11. mč-á+ [*second conjugation even though* ns-A,
              since h-A *type takes precedence*]

12. sp-ă̆+ [*second conjugation; mutation in first*
              singular, nonpast]

13. sl-á+ [*V+V mutation occurs and takes the form* sl → šļ]

14. čţ-í+ [*no V+V mutation*]

15. u-m̦ertv̦-í+ [*V+V mutation takes the form* tv̦ → ščvļ]

16. roḑ-í+ [*when perfective, past tense has shifting stress*]

17. roḑ-í+șa [*when perfective, there is optional end stress:* роди́лся́, роди́ла́сь роди́ло́сь, роди́ли́сь]

Three verbs present a mixture of conjugational types:

1. xoţ-é+ [*second and third singular, nonpast from* xot-ǎ+]

2. h̦ež-á+ [*first singular and third plural of nonpast, imperative, and present active verbal adjective from* h̦eg+]

3. -šíb+ [*infinitive and past passive verbal adjective from* -šib̦-ǐ+]

Two verbs are anomalous in their nonpast tense forms:

1. dǎj+ [*nonpast tense:* да́м, да́шь, да́ст, дади́м, дади́те, даду́т; *imperative:* да́й; *past passive verbal adjective uses formant* -n]

2. jéd+ [*nonpast tense:* е́м, е́шь, е́ст, еди́м, еди́те, едя́т; *imperative:* е́шь]

INDEX

LIST OF EXERCISES

A NOTE ON SOURCES

In addition to the works by Halle, Lipson, and Townsend already referred to in the preface (p. vi), the reference works listed below were consulted in the writing of this book. On questions of word stress or the acceptability of certain forms, I have generally followed Avanesov and Ožegov. In those instances when that work did not provide information, Barxudarov or the Academy dictionary were used.

Akademija nauk SSSR. *Slovar' russkogo jazyka.* 4 vols. M.: GIINS, 1957-61.

Avanesov, R. I. and S. I. Ožegov (eds.). *Russkoe literaturnoe proiznošenie i udarenie. Slovar'- spravočnik.* M.: GIINS, 1959.

Barxudarov, S. G. *et al.* (eds.). *Orfografičeskij slovar' russkogo jazyka.* 8th ed. M.: Sovetskaja Ènciklopedija, 1968.

Gribble, Charles E. *Russian Root List with a Sketch of Word Formation.* Cambridge, Mass.: Slavica, 1973.

Lazova, M. V. (ed.). *Obratnyj slovar' russkogo jazyka.* M.: Sovetskaja Ènciklopedija, 1974.

Red'kin, V. A. *Akcentologija sovremennogo russkogo literaturnogo jazyka.* M.: Prosveščenie, 1971.

Unbegaun, Boris. *Russian Grammar.* Oxford: Clarendon Press, 1957.

Vasmer, Max. *Ètimologičeskij slovar' russkogo jazyka. Perevod s nemeckogo i dopolnenija O. N. Trubačeva.* 4 vols. M.: Progress, 1964-73.

Vinogradov, V. V. *et al.* (eds.). *Grammatika russkogo jazyka.* Vol. 1: *Fonetika i morfologija.* M.: AN SSSR, 1960 [rpt.].

Zaliznjak, A. A. *Russkoe imennoe slovoizmenenie.* M.: Nauka, 1967.

BOOKS FROM SLAVICA PUBLISHERS

American Contributions to the Eighth International Congress of Slavists, Volume 1: Linguistics and Poetics, ed. by Henrik Birnbaum, 818 p., 1978; *Volume 2: Literature*, ed. by Victor Terras, 799 p., 1978.

Henrik Birnbaum: *Common Slavic Progress and Problems in Its Reconstruction*, xi + 436 p., 1975.

Malcolm H. Brown, ed.: *Papers of the Yugoslav-American Seminar on Music*, 208 p., 1970.

Ellen B. Chances: *Conformity's Children: An Approach to the Superfluous Man in Russian Literature*, 1978.

Catherine V. Chvany: *On the Syntax of Be-Sentences in Russian*, viii + 311 p., 1975.

Frederick Columbus: *Introductory Workbook in Historical Phonology*, 39 p., 1974.

Dina B. Crockett: *Agreement in Contemporary Standard Russian*, iv + 456 p., 1976.

Paul Debreczeny and Thomas Eekman, eds.: *Chekhov's Art of Writing A Collection of Critical Essays*, 199 p., 1977.

Ralph Carter Elwood, ed.: *Reconsiderations on the Russian Revolution*, x + 278 p., 1976. (Papers from the Banff '74 Conference)

Folia Slavica, a journal, first issue March 1977.

Richard Freeborn, R. R. Milner-Gulland, and Charles A. Ward, eds.: *Russian and Slavic Literature*, xii + 466 p., 1976. (Papers from the Banff '74 Conference)

Victor A. Friedman: *The Grammatical Categories of the Macedonian Indicative*, 210 p., 1977.

Charles E. Gribble, ed.: *Medieval Slavic Texts, Vol. 1, Old and Middle Russian Texts*, 320 p., 1973.

Charles E. Gribble: *Russian Root List with a Sketch of Russian Word Formation*, 56 p., 1973.

BOOKS FROM SLAVICA PUBLISHERS

Charles E. Gribble: Словарик русского языка 18-го века/*A Short Dictionary of 18th-Century Russian*, 103 p., 1976.

Charles E. Gribble, ed.: *Studies Presented to Professor Roman Jakobson by His Students*, 333 p., 1968.

Pierre Hart: *The Life and Work of Gavriil Derzhavin*, 1978.

Raina Katzarova-Kukudova & Kiril Djenev: *Bulgarian Folk Dances*, 174 p., numerous illustrations, 2nd printing 1976 (1st printing, Sofia 1958).

Demetrius J. Koubourlis, ed.: *Topics in Slavic Phonology*, viii + 270 p., 1974.

Michael K. Launer: *Elementary Russian Syntax*, xi + 140 p., 1974.

Jules F. Levin: *Reading Contemporary Russian*, 1978.

Maurice I. Levin: *Russian Declension and Conjugation, A Structural Description with Exercises*, x + 160 p., 1978.

Alexander Lipson: *A Russian Course*.

Paul Macura: *Russian-English Botanical Dictionary*, 1979.

Thomas F. Magner, ed.: *Slavic Linguistics and Language Teaching*, x + 309 p., 1976. (Papers from the Banff '74 Conference)

Mateja Matejić and Dragan Milivojevic: *An Anthology of Medieval Serbian Literature*, 1978.

Mateja Matejić and others: *A Handbook of Bulgarian Authors*, 1979.

Vasa D. Mihailovich and Mateja Matejić: *Yugoslav Literature in English A Bibliography of Translations and Criticism (1821-1975)*, ix + 328 p., 1976.

Kenneth E. Naylor, ed.: *Balkanistica: Occasional Papers in Southeast European Studies*, I(1974), 189 p., 1975; II(1975), 153 p., 1976; III(1976), 155 p., 1978.

BOOKS FROM SLAVICA PUBLISHERS

Lawrence W. Newman: *A Comprehensive Russian Grammar by A. A. Barsov*, 1979.

Felix J. Oinas, ed.: *Folklore Nationalism & Politics*, 190 p., 1977.

Hongor Oulanoff: *The Prose Fiction of Veniamin A. Kaverin*, v + 203 p., 1976.

Papers in Slovene Studies, ed. by Rudolf M. Susel, Number 3, 1978.

Jan L. Perkowski, ed.: *Vampires of the Slavs* (a collection of readings), 294 p., 1976.

T. M. S. Priestly and Bruce Derwing: *Reading Rules for Russian*, 1979.

Lester A. Rice: *Hungarian Morphological Irregularities*, 80 p., 1970.

Midhat Ridjanović: *A Synchronic Study of Verbal Aspect in English and Serbo-Croatian*, ix + 147 p., 1976.

David F. Robinson: *Lithuanian Reverse Dictionary*, ix + 209 p., 1976.

Don K. Rowney and G. Edward Orchard, eds.: *Russian and Slavic History*, viii + 311 p., 1977. (Papers from the Banff '74 Conference)

Ernest A. Scatton: *Bulgarian Phonology*, xii + 224 p., 1976.

William R. Schmalstieg: *Introduction to Old Church Slavic*, 290 p., 1976.

Michael Shapiro: *Aspects of Russian Morphology, A Semiotic Investigation*, 62 p., 1969.

Charles E. Townsend: *Czech Through Russian*, 1979.

Charles E. Townsend: *The Memoirs of Princess Natal'ja Borisovna Dolgorukaja*, viii + 146 p., 1977.

Charles E. Townsend: *Russian Word-Formation, corrected reprint*, xviii + 272 p., 1975.

BOOKS FROM SLAVICA PUBLISHERS

D. N. Ushakov, ed.: Толковый словарь русского языка,
original edition in 4 volumes, Moscow, 1934-1940;
reprint (slightly reduced in page size, corrections indicated throughout, 4 volumes bound in
3), 1974.

Daniel C. Waugh: *The Great Turk's Correspondence*,
1979.

Susan Wobst: *Russian Readings & Grammar Terminology*,
88 p., 1978.

Dean S. Worth: *A Bibliography of Russian Word-
Formation*, xliv + 317 p., 1977.

Eng 212 -1   306 -/
Fredericka   Kroll